Learning Community

Finding Common Ground in Difference

Learning Community

Finding Common Ground in Difference

PATRICIA E. CALDERWOOD

Teachers College, Columbia University
New York and London

Published by Teachers College Press, 1234 Amsterdam Avenue, New York, NY 10027

Library of Congress Cataloging-in-Publication Data

Calderwood, Patricia E., 1954–
   Learning community : finding common ground in difference / Patricia E. Calderwood.
      p. cm.
   Includes bibliographical references and index.
   ISBN 0-8077-3953-7 (cloth)—ISBN 0-8077-3952-9 (pbk.)
      1. Group work in education—United States.   2. Group identity—United States.   3. Interpersonal relations—United States.   I. Title.
   LB1032.C34 2000
   370.11—dc21   00-024926

ISBN 0-8077-3952-9 (paper)
ISBN 0-8077-3953-7 (cloth)

Printed on acid-free paper

Manufactured in the United States of America

07 06 05 04 03 02 01 00   8 7 6 5 4 3 2 1

Contents

Preface

When I first tell colleagues, school administrators, or teachers about my interest in community, I find myself flinching as I brace for the inevitable request that follows. "Can you give us a workshop on community?" My response has always been, and probably will continue to be, "No, I cannot." I suspect they think that I am a charlatan, pretending an expertise I do not have. They do not seem to believe that I have not found a formula that will conjure the highly desirable state of community for them. Perhaps they are simply disappointed to learn that a workshop cannot jump-start the practices, social relations, and feelings that coalesce to form community.

As we see in the following pages, community isn't always as lovely in practice as it may be in our dreams. This is because what we know as community is cobbled together, deliberately or inadvertently, by ordinary and imperfect people. Despite the imperfections, I would still choose to work and learn in a school suffused with community rather than in one that echoed with its absence. I am not alone in this preference.

This book is an attempt to tell what I have learned about community from students and teachers who have welcomed me into their circles. During the research projects from which I draw my information, people talked and wrote about community—about its meanings, about its presence or absence in their school, and the evidence they used to make the distinction (Blot & Calderwood, 1995; Calderwood, 1997). I examined practices of community in four school settings: a public urban college, a private Catholic elementary school, an all-girls private Catholic high school, and an urban public middle school. This exploration of the relationship between vulnerability, fragility, and resilience of community may provide educators with some indication of what might be possible regarding the support of the practices, social relations, and feelings of community in schools.

ACKNOWLEDGMENTS

The Bruner Foundation and the Facilitator Center of New York underwrote two of the studies upon which I have based this book, for which I am very grateful. Fairfield University supported the final revisions with a timely and much appreciated summer stipend. The journals *Urban Education* and *The*

Urban Review have given their permission to include excerpts from essays they have published (Calderwood, 1998a, in press-a, and in press-b).

Of the many relevant topics I could have chosen to examine, only that of community resonated deeply within my own being. As an habitual outsider, I cherish the few affiliative bonds that draw me into fellowship with others. I am infinitely grateful to my advisors, friends, and family who wove the bonds of community with me: Richard Blot, Michelle Fine, Frederick Erickson, David Fletcher, Jennifer McCormick, Kathleen McDermott, and Ken, Jonathan, David, and Emily Rolston.

Many children, women, and men shared their lives and dreams with me during the course of the various projects. Although they must remain unnamed here, I thank them all and acknowledge their invaluable contributions. I sincerely hope that I have done justice to their trust.

CHAPTER 1

Examining Community

THE CALL FOR COMMUNITY IN SCHOOL

People believe in community. It is not only a cherished notion of close-knit humanity but also a fundamental expression of the cooperative human social activity that ensures our survival as a species. Connection, caring, interdependence, shared values, rituals and celebrations, the security of being known, of belonging to a group, of being significant—these images, among many others, come to mind when one thinks about community. Within our complex society, the social relations of community mitigate against anonymity and humanize our institutions. The infusion of a sense of community, in fact, is often suggested as a remedy when our institutions cannot effectively function as we desire. Resilient community is celebrated not only because it enhances our humanity but because many people believe that other worthy ends can be accomplished best in the presence of community. This longing for and celebration of community as a means to achieving important goals is pervasive in our schools.

However, whether the attempts at building community and a sense of community are successful or fail in schools may depend on factors that cannot be entirely anticipated or controlled. Every school is different. The idea of community will likely mean something different at each school, and the social relations and practices of community will proceed and be understood uniquely at every school, if they are there at all. Likewise, if there are no practices or social relations that engender community at a particular school, there will be practices and social relations that engender the absence of community. There will always be schools in which the participants move in and out of being in community with each other.

If the presence or absence of community affects the ways that schools and schooling function, as current research indicates, and if the presence of community is a positive force, it may seem tempting to invent a way to inoculate schools with a sense of community—and to inject them with the conditions within which community might be sustained. The literature on effective schools and on school reform relies heavily on the notion that community is a necessary element of successful schools and of school transformation (Lieberman, 1992, 1994; McQuillan & Muncie, 1994; Newmann, Rutter, & Smith, 1989;

1

Sizer, 1992). There is also a body of research that suggests or explores the relationship between student outcomes and the presence of community in schools. This research posits a strong positive relationship between successful student outcomes and community but falls short of establishing any causal relationship (Blot & Calderwood, 1995; Bryk, Lee, & Holland, 1993; Coleman & Hoffer, 1987).

Sergiovanni (1994), among others, writes about the desirability of nurturing, supportive communal relations in schools in contrast to those more contractual, hierarchical, and impersonal relations frequently found in educational institutions. A sincere belief in the inherent goodness and desirability of communal relations in schooling drives his work. The social relations of community are similar to those evoked as necessary for desirable middle school configurations (Lipsitz, 1984; Oakes, Quartz, Gong, Guiton, & Lipton, 1993). They also figure prominently in the elements of effective school climates and organizations in traditional quantitative studies of school success (Newmann et al., 1989; Sizer, 1992). Coleman and Hoffer (1987), Sergiovanni (1994), and Westheimer (1998) provide the few exceptional examples in the education literature that provide more than a brief exposition of the meanings of community. In general, however, education researchers and practitioners take the notion for granted as they explain school climate and success or call for its reorganization or transformation.

Because the call to transform schools into "real" communities is so widespread, critical and reflective inquiry about the nature of community is necessary. As stated earlier, the temptation to inoculate schools with community, if only one could, is strong. Community, however, is a slippery state of social relations. It is not a commodity easily obtained. There is no storehouse stocking tempting varieties and flavors of ready-made community, nor is there a warehouse filled with the ingredients that, when properly arranged, transform into community. Community gets built only as community is practiced, and successful construction of resilient community is not guaranteed, even among the most dedicated group. Resilient community can elude a group intent on its construction, even as it might blossom unexpectedly as another group carries out some different enterprise.

Although the practices of community, the habitual or customary activities, social relations, values, and beliefs that people refer to when they speak of community, are understood and played out distinctly within different groups, a common set of conditions exists that must be met if the social relations of community are to produce resilient and enduring community. These conditions are centered in the creation and maintenance of meaningful differences and commonalities. In other words, the social relations of community are grounded in individuated and group identity.

Common sense, wistfulness, and communitarians tell us that the most basic task of community is to strengthen commonalities within its membership. The allure of commonality, however, obscures a more fundamental and essential task. The basic task of community is not to make common but rather to differentiate, that is, to account for the differentiation of insiders from outsiders and of insiders from each other. For community to become resilient and to flourish, the members need to attend to the vulnerabilities that accompany the accommodation of these differences. This work can be accomplished if the group operates under the following conditions (Blot & Calderwood, 1995; Calderwood, 1997):

For a social group to be in community there must be a belief that they in fact share identity, beliefs, values, norms, practices, history and goals specific and unique to the group and distinguishable from those of other social groups.

There need to be actual times and events which celebrate a sense of being in community, including celebrations marking entering or exiting community membership or changing status within the community.

Competent membership within community must be learned.

Existing or potential differences between competing values, beliefs and practices within the group must be recognized, reconciled or tolerated.

For any group that wishes to maintain itself in community, it is important that their practices are such that the above conditions arise and persevere. If the conditions are sufficiently present, then it will be possible to carry out the work of differentiation, to attend to its concomitant vulnerabilities, and to perhaps build resilient community.

Because community is such a fragile state, the ways that group members heed its vulnerabilities are of paramount concern. Resilience is created and strengthened because vulnerabilities and fragilities offer the opportunity to develop the habits and practices that protect and deepen the social relations of community. This is counterintuitive to the notion that community within a group is strong because commonalities indicate strength and resilience.

As will become evident, there are many ways to describe or use the label *community* when considering the practices and social relations of particular social groups. The analyses of what these ordinary people do, say, and believe about community demonstrate that although the idea of community often seems clear and easy to know, its purposes and practices have specific local meanings held together by multiple and sometimes contradictory understandings.

VULNERABILITY, FRAGILITY, AND RESILIENCE IN COMMUNITY

The relation between vulnerability and resilience is fundamental to the workings of community. In other words, resilience is predicated upon the existence of vulnerability. Community without vulnerability is impoverished as to the opportunity to carry out the responsive practices that build resilience. Community untested by vulnerability is neither here nor there, neither weak nor strong. But strength and fragility as elements of the practices of community, as qualities of community, do not exist independently or concretely outside these practices, nor do they lie dormant until called up. Strength and resilience are ephemeral—real and relevant only as the social relations of community play out. Strength in one context may be fragility in another. Resilience is a possible response to vulnerability, fragility is another possible response to vulnerability, and fragility can sometimes be developed into the strength of resilience. Certain responses to vulnerabilities in community, then, offer practice in resilience. Other responses do not and may lead to the development of community-threatening fragility. What happens with vulnerability is more reliably indicative of the resilience or fragility of community than is how smoothly that community's social relations and practices proceed.

The work of creating and sustaining individuated identity and group identity in community can reveal or create vulnerabilities as well as strengths. If vulnerabilities are perceived as design flaws, or as cracks undermining the strength of a foundation, they may be attended to as dangers imperiling the well-being of community. Groups and their members might act precipitously to eradicate the perceived dangers without a full understanding of the opportunities they present to build resilience. Perhaps vulnerabilities are perceived as trivial or inconsequential, and thus ignored or tolerated. Even vulnerabilities viewed as extremely threatening may be ignored or tolerated, perhaps because the community is in denial or because it lacks any other method to attend to them. Even when vulnerabilities are noticed, examined, and attended to with the intention of building resilience, resilience is not always achieved. Sometimes the vulnerabilities prove fatal to the health of community despite all efforts.

At times, sustaining community in school is challenged and sometimes threatened by differences or tensions within. For example, communities invent their own heterogeneity and differences within, even when they look homogeneous from the outside. Differences in roles, social status, and power, even when taken for granted, are important within community. However these differences are configured, whether justly or unjustly, they affect community. Each time differences are explicitly laid out and examined, opportunities for strengthening or fracturing the community are available to be chosen. Those in community may choose to tolerate potential or actual instances of fracture, if these are balanced by instances of community strengthening. The strength of community can in part be measured by the extent to which fractures heal while collaborative strengths are sustained.

DESCRIBING COMMUNITY

Although the notion of community is important in schools, all too often the assumption is made that everyone knows and agrees about what community is and what communities look like. Community, then, is sometimes thought of as a thing, a commodity, rather than as a label used to describe certain sets of social configurations and social relations (Blot, personal communication, 1995). Thinking of community as a commodity leads to the call to inoculate schools. However, inquiry that explores what community means and how it works may be far more useful to school transformation or effectiveness than any attempts to inject community therapeutically. If we are to resist the tendency to regard community as a commodity, we should pay attention to the situationally specific, context-bound conditions within which community can occur. We need to focus on the social practices that bring about the social relations and the feelings about them that we call community and sense of community.

One of the difficulties encountered when one writes or talks about community is directly related to the utilitarian tendency of devising catchall constructs and categories, symbols, to explain complex phenomena that we assume are universally understood by all with whom we communicate (Mead, 1934). The symbol, because of its presumed accessibility, stands in for a complicated set of understandings of phenomena while actually glossing over them in the service of communicative ease. Hence we find it all but impossible to refrain from referring to "community" as "it" because "it" has become simply a word, a pronoun—a convenient symbol that we have come to accept. However, we then find ourselves thinking of community as a simple thing rather than as the complex and rather messy sets of practices and beliefs that the symbol represents.

Consequently, it is important to recognize that what community means and how it works differs from group to group and setting to setting. Indeed, within any one group or setting, we are likely to find multiple opportunities to call what we see or feel community. Conditions that may seem important in one setting may be irrelevant, nonexistent, or impossible to sustain in another (Blot & Calderwood, 1995).

The root of the term *community* is derived from the Latin word *communis*, and in its earliest and most enduring sense links *under obligation* with *together* (Williams, 1976). The social transactions that mark the process of community are conducted among differentiated individuals within the social group. Logically, then, some accounting must be made of these individuals in order that those within community can know how to transact effectively with each other. They must "communicate," that is, talk together and construct shared meanings. In addition, according to Glare (1990), the root word *munio* means "to provide with defensive fortifications" or "to build a fortified town." Thus those in community (*communis*) together construct the walls or boundaries that ward off outsiders. The work of community, then, from the earliest use of the term, has always incorporated the mutual processes of inclusion and exclusion, marked by the construction and defense of borders or boundaries and internal transactions of talk and other social relations among differentiated individuals (Erickson, personal communication, 1996). The organization of community is based on symbolic behavior in the form of beliefs, values, and activities that reflect the social relations we call community (Cohen, 1985; Hillary, 1955, 1986).

The word *community* has two important meanings in current popular usage: It labels specific groups of people and describes specific social relations among people within a social group. A group may consider itself to be a community or may be labeled as such by outsiders. Certain types of social relations may be pointed out (again, by insider or outsider) as indicative of the presence of community within the group.

Conceptions of community are multiple because community is constituted, sustained, enriched, and transformed by the relationships and shared meanings among its members. Social constructions such as community are the utilization of certain practices that sustain, challenge, support, and transform social relations (Blot & Calderwood, 1995). As any particular social reality is contingent rather than given, change or stasis is a result of interaction between existing social structure and human agency and choice, however constrained that agency and choice may be by factors such as history and available resources. The social construction of community within any particular group is contingent on the group's social reality as well as the meanings it assigns to that social reality; simultaneously, local understandings of community help construct and define social reality for the group.

People are drawn together into community through various means and for various reasons. The existence of geographic proximity, economic interdependence, or shared values and beliefs are common cohering factors.

Geographically bounded, or value-centered, or religiously affiliated social groups are often called communities. Often, the people living within a particular neighborhood are considered by themselves and others to be a community, although affirmation of one's membership in, and sense of belonging to, a neighborhood-based community is sometimes dependent upon the degree of its geographic isolation (Cuba, 1993; Puddifoot, 1993). Such communities are often economically based and revolve primarily around the allocation of resources and goods, including education (Coleman & Hoffer, 1987; Hillary, 1955, 1959, 1986; Minar & Greer, 1969; Nisbet, 1953; Stein, 1960; Tönnies, 1988/1887). The groups share certain characteristics that include common beliefs, values, goals, and practices embedded within a network of supportive and positive social relationships. An explicit understanding of what community means in general or specific circumstances is not always present.

Social scientists have set up ideal types such as community and society to explain how some social groups operate (Gusfield, 1975; Tönnies, 1988/1887). Simple versus complex, preindustrial versus industrial, intimate versus distant, commitment versus contract, innocent versus worldly—the schemas evoke images in stark contrast to each other, an either-or set. Society is hierarchical, technical, held together by contracts and laws. Community, in contrast, is based on kinship and commitment. Over time, these oppositions have taken on evaluative tones that tend to imply that community social relations are more authentic, pure, and desirable than societal social relations, which are in turn seen as contrived, artificial, and alienating.

Benedict Anderson (1991), in *Imagined Communities*, traces the birth of national and colonial identities over the past centuries. The possibility of imagining community that transcends immediate geographical proximity arose as production and distribution of mass communication through technological innovation grew. Suddenly, factors other than close kinship or immediacy of geography seeped into personal and group identity. Widespread communication through shared print language made it possible to include hitherto unknown others in one's social group, on the basis of presumed shared worldviews, language, customs, and so on, extending the idea of family kinship into the idea of nation. We are Americans, then, for example, not only because we connect through shared institutions such as government but also because we have inherited, acquired, or invented an individual and collective identity that imagines shared traits, characteristics, and worldviews uniquely American. Similarly, we find it possible to imagine ourselves in global community with countless others, on the basis of shared religious beliefs, political affiliations, professions, genders, and so on. Still, within the imaginings that have freed community from its kin and geographical boundaries lies the challenge of accounting for and accommodating the existence of persistent and pervasive diversity.

The structure of community exists, harmoniously or in discord, with the social relationships of its members. The meanings ascribed to the practices of community transform or maintain the practices intact, even as the ongoing social construction of the meanings does depend in part on how historical and existing practices and contexts circumscribe the scope of possible meanings. As an illustration, let us look at the convergence and divergence of two categories of community often examined by sociologists, the values and functional communities.

Values Community

Shared values and beliefs often draw people together and move them to act as a community (Bellah, Madsen, Sullivan, Swindler, & Tipton, 1985; Minar & Greer, 1969). The articulations of community within an institution, a school perhaps, may resound particularly strongly, and that institution may consequently become labeled, and thought of, as a community in its own right. For example, Bryk et al. (1993) in *Catholic Schools and the Common Good* report that students and teachers alike described their Catholic high schools as communities. "We are a community" was a common refrain in the responses to their inquiries about how people perceived themselves within the context of their schools (p. 275).

Membership in the values community is voluntary, even within values communities with relatively impermeable borders that separate insider from outsider. Some values communities are created and sustained by those groups, such as the Amish, who, for philosophical or religious reasons, set themselves apart from mainstream society. Such values communities bear some resemblance to Goffman's (1961) total institutions in their clarity of border between inside and outside. Those who move between inside and outside in these values communities maintain a consistent social identity as always either insiders or outsiders of the community. The mere act of commerce does not alter this social identification. Engaging in commerce with outsiders does not affect an insider's belonging to the group, although it may lead to a uniquely defined role within the group. Engaging in commerce with the group does not impart group membership or insider identity to the outsider, although there may be a role at the periphery of the group for the outsider.

Many value-centered institutions or groups do not require total commitment of values, practices, and beliefs from their members. Magnet schools, private schools, and alternative schools are examples of such value-centered institutions. Such institutions exist in service to the shared values of the members and are often created in response to those values. They do not necessarily develop in the members a sense of community that carries over and permeates every social relation, practice, belief, or value. Because each member may hold other values harmonious or discordant with those that they communally share, this kind of values community, then, is relevant to only some aspects of a member's life, even if its members would like to believe otherwise. Even as such institutions arise in response to shared values, they can create a sheltering umbrella under which community and a sense of community can flourish. The institution is symbolic of the cohering values and purposes of the group—which may or may not be in community. For example, when Catholic high school students told Bryk et al. (1993) that their schools were communities, school was a symbol of their community and not "the community."

Functional Communities

Coleman and Hoffer (1987) write that "structural consistency between generations creates what can be described as a functional community, a community in which social norms and sanctions, including those that cross generations, arise out of the social structure itself, and both reinforce and perpetuate that structure" (p. 7). There is one system of values and beliefs that is dominant in a functional community (Coleman & Hoffer, 1987; Minar & Greer, 1969). Deviance from these dominant beliefs and values is tolerated only to the degree that such deviance does not overtly challenge practices. Stigmatization and sanctions are the lot of those whose practices reveal deviant values. Norms ensure not only that members live out the values of the community but that newcomers and less expert members learn how to be in community. Although a traditional functional community, such as an isolated small town, encompasses every aspect of the community members' lives, every functional community need not do so to that extent. The functional community of which the Catholic schools are institutions, for example, is organized around the values and beliefs of the Catholic religion. It is primarily a spiritual or faith community.

A faith community is another type of functional community. Faith communities cohere around distinct religious beliefs, including recognition of pervasive spiritual community. A faith community is not locally bound, although there are local clusters of faith community members, such as temple congregations and parish churches. Locally specific practices and norms may vary, but the essential core of beliefs and values is universal within the faith community.

Religious schools serve widespread functional communities whose local populations are only incidentally bound by geography, language, social customs, and so on. The functional community is a spiritually focused faith community; accidents of geography, ethnicity, and so on, are incidental to the core of values and beliefs around which the community coalesces. A spiritual community shares two essential elements: The members are kin within a spiritual family, and they share a belief in a supreme spiritual being. For the believers all humanity is inescapably within spiritual community, for the spiritual is an essential element of being human. In Catholic schools, the students are told by their teachers that they are "children of God"—a reference to the spiritual community of which even nonbelievers are members.

There are important elements that distinguish functional communities from values communities. One is the intergenerational membership of the functional community, which takes many years to evolve. Another is that, in a values community, common values and beliefs draw members into community with each other. If what is common changes or dissipates over time, so does the nature of the practices of community of the group. A values community falls apart or transforms when values change or erode. In contrast, the dominant, cohering set of beliefs and values in a functional community stands unchanged over time, supported by rigorous adherence to the group's norms. Values communities can, over time, become functional communities as the acceptable practices of community become entrenched over generations.

We have already seen that some schools are institutions of values communities. Similarly, they can also be institutions of functional communities. In a small town or village, for example, the school supports, through the generations, the norms, values, and particular social structure of the community. However, in some cases, the functional community that instituted the school or educational system has changed in fundamental ways, although the school continues to operate. The composition of the membership may have changed, values and norms may have altered or eroded, an established tradition of successive generations of families attending the local school may have been interrupted by immigration patterns, and so on. The school's practices may remain static or may adjust to accommodate the population it now serves. Even when a functional community is no longer in place, the school can become an institution that serves a collection of people who live in an area.

Catholic and other religious schools, when faced with the changes described above, may continue to exist as institutions within functional communities. The functional communities that they serve are affected only in minor ways by population changes, technological advances, and so on. The core of values and beliefs, and most of the normative sanctions, do not substantially differ with the population. They continue, essentially unchanged and unassailable.

The preceding paragraphs outline some structural and functional aspects of community, elements that shape some of the practices of the groups discussed in this study. However, the meaningfulness of practices of community are not possible to understand simply by examining labels and categories. Every instance of human social activity holds meaning and intention and consequences. In order to understand what community means to its makers then, we must seek to understand its practices in ways that undo the overly simplistic labels and categories designed by social scientists.

Beyond Communitarian Thought

Bellah et al. (1985) in *Habits of the Heart* write of the desire of Americans to create and sustain the communitarian nature of an idealized America. The interconnectedness and mutual dependency that are hallmarks of community are understood as essentially human connections, without which we are diminished human beings.

Bellah et al. (1985) attribute much of the absence of what they consider as "true" community in our society to the development of a cult of individualism, the elevation of the rights, needs, and desires of individuals over those of a group. This has to a great extent eradicated or distorted the recognition of the nature and necessity of mutual commitment and dependence (Nisbet, 1953; Stein, 1960). In contemporary America, the ability to sustain committed, mutually dependent relationships has become largely the work of families.

Bellah et al. (1985) describe the elements of what they call "community of memory." Communities of memory, embodied in individuals, learn who they are as they continue to create who they are as a community. They remember their shared past, continually retell its stories, create heroes and villains, and participate in practices that affirm the community. Such a community of memory is also then a community of hope for its own future. It envisions its future because it understands its goals, beliefs, and practices and acts to sustain these.

Amitai Etzioni (1993) outlines a communitarian philosophy and code of action, which is intended to compensate for what he considers a dangerous overemphasis on individual rights, entitlements and privileges that have all but eliminated a sense of shared responsibility and commitment to all. Reestablishing norms and inventing laws that protect the interests of the American community as a whole, he writes, is a priority. The subordination and even sacrifice of individual rights is, he believes, a small but necessary cost of this adjustment. He believes that the very survival of American society is dependent upon such a shift in priorities.

Communitarians, according to Frazer and Lacey (1993), set up the idea of community as a therapeutic antidote to and necessary correction of perceived present-day societal ills by creating a paradigm that places personal rights and entitlements in opposition to "the greater good" served by a nationwide sense of communal responsibility. Current critiques (Knight-Abowitz, 1997; Moon, 1993; Phillips, 1993) of communitarian thought, represented above by Bellah et al. (1985) and Etzioni (1993), demonstrate that the communitarians long for reinstitution of "lost" community that has never existed without extensive exclusionary practices (Dewey, 1969; Minar & Greer, 1969; Tönnies, 1988/1887). The "common good," as shown by Frazer and Lacey (1993), Moon (1993), Phillips (1993), and Tinder (1980), often still means what is good only for the powerful or elite within a social group and often can be achieved only at the expense of the less powerful and marginalized members of the group.

We don't live in ideal communities, as the critics of communitarianism argue, for there is an inherent tension between individual freedom and mutually supportive coexistence. There is an ambivalence about how much we really want to live in community, given this uneasy relationship. The balancing of personal rights and entitlements with the "common good" is an inherent, irreducible tension within our society and within social groups striving to achieve community (Knight-Abowitz, 1997). We need to imagine that there are ideal communities toward which we work in order to imagine ways to reconcile the tensions (Mandelbaum, 1988). According to Frazer and Lacey (1993), Knight-Abowitz (1997), Moon (1993), and Tinder (1980), we need to address issues of plurality, diversity, and power within and across communities.

Building Identity

As noted earlier, what is important about community is that it is based on symbolic behavior. The symbolic construction of community is accomplished by ensuring that the group is apart from and different from other social groups through the establishment of a group identity recognizable from within and outside the group (Cohen, 1985, 1994; Epstein, 1992; Hillary, 1986; Smiley, 1992).

Community has symbolic boundaries and symbolic borders, which demarcate the inclusion or exclusion of what and who constitute the frame of reference for this construction of identity. They mark out with whom one is affiliated or from whom one is distant (Blot, personal communication, 1995; Cohen, 1985). These symbolic boundaries and borders are permeable and moveable, continually adjusted in the ebb and flow of social relations. The control of boundaries that delineate identity within community is routinely accomplished in the ordinary activities, beliefs, and language of people. A conscious intention of delineating community identity may be manifest but quite often is not.

It may be useful to consider the concept of boundary as like the skin of one's own sense of individual and group identity. It symbolizes who one is, and who one is not. The boundaries of community comprise the "face" presented to outsiders, its collective public identity (following Goffman, 1959). The collective construction of boundaries that mark out those within community from those outside is essentially similar to the marking out of self from other in the individual. It is a protective action, used to protect the purity and integrity of the individual or collective body from the impure defilement of some generalized other (Sibley, 1995).

Frederick Erickson (1987), who in turn credits Barth (1969), notes a difference between cultural boundary and cultural border, a distinction that holds for the borders and boundaries of community. Boundaries are of themselves politically neutral, but borders are politicized areas thrown up to defend boundaries. Sibley's (1995) use of the term boundaries is closely aligned with the notion of politicized border—the space where value judgments about insider/outsider are weighted and the power to include or exclude is exercised. Cohen (1985) remarks that "members find their identities as individuals through their occupancy of the community's social space: if outsiders trespass in that space, then its occupants' own sense of self is felt to be debased and defaced" (p.109).

People invest in boundaries and borders, and work to maintain them or create them because of their important utility in the constitution of a sense of an individuated, selectively affiliated self (Cohen, 1994; Epstein, 1992; Mead, 1934). The permeability and subjective nature of community border and boundary are illustrated in Robinson's 1994 analysis of "passing," or the successful pretense of in-group membership by an otherwise outcast. Such passing makes the borders and boundaries of a community visible to the transgressors and to the transgressed. In accepting the passer as one of their own, the community members draw the borders around who belongs and create the boundaries of their self and group identification. Transgression of the borders is only possible if their existence is acknowledged. In this way, for the outsider who "passes," it is both victory over the insiders and submission to their terms. The borders and boundaries are created and sustained in the acknowledgment, while simultaneously in the transgressions they may be eroded or redrawn.

Inclusion and Exclusion

An important element in the creation of group identity is the negotiation of inclusion and exclusion. A number of considerations influence such decisions. One significant issue is that of justice.

Social psychologists have studied and written extensively about considerations of justice in using the practices of inclusion and exclusion to delineate social groups. Opotow (1990) writes that "moral values, rules, and considerations of fairness apply only to those within this boundary for fairness, called our 'scope of justice' or 'moral community'" (p. 3). She explains that there is a

> coherent cluster of attitudes that comprised moral inclusion: (1) believing that considerations of fairness apply to another, (2) willingness to allocate a share of community resources to another, and (3) willingness to make sacrifices to foster another's well-being. (p. 4)

Deutch (1990), Fine (1990), and Opotow (1990) discuss how belonging, connection, identity, and social exclusion can be created and sustained by individuals within groups. Simply, moral community is a "boundary for fairness" (Opotow, 1990), the "map" of the practices of communal interrelationship. Moral community is inclusive for those for whom one feels a sense of caring and commitment. Value judgments about the worth of individuals or groups and about the nature and quality of their connection to oneself or one's group determine membership and exclusion. It is common to exclude individuals or groups from one's moral community. Ginsberg (1994) makes the argument that the greater one is removed in space and, more important, in time, from others, the more diminished is his or her sense of caring responsibility to those others. This predilection to exclude others from one's moral community is seen by social psychologists as an underlying mechanism for many social injustices.

Conversely, the ability of people to expand their moral community often occurs in conjunction with practices that demonstrate recognition of the responsibility for the welfare of a fellow member of one's community (Frazer & Lacey, 1993; Moon, 1993; Phillips, 1993; Warren, 1969). Similarly, the philosopher Smiley (1992) examines the determining importance of perceived communal boundaries on the presence or absence of the feeling of moral responsibility for the existence of social inequity or injustice. The recognition of one's individual or group privileged status constructed in relationship with another's deprivation can impel one to act to eradicate the injustice if the boundaries of care and concern open to include the other person or group.

With regard to the notion of social group boundaries, Wolfe (1992) notes a tension between postmodern and democratic ideals and sociological necessity. Because differences can, and often are, created or utilized to justify and carry out social injustices, they are seemingly incompatible with the democratic ideals of equality and justice. However, as he states: "Exclusion, however difficult to justify, is what makes diversity possible, societies interesting, institutions necessary, practices creative, customs variable, and ambiguity important" (p. 312). The tension between the risks and benefits of inclusion and exclusion signified by boundaries and borders demands thoughtful consideration (Gans, 1992). If the boundaries are strenuously maintained by insiders who seek only to protect their own privilege without consideration for their responsibilities for the consequences to others, for example, then those boundaries are fair game for demolition. Such a consideration resonates with what Harding (1991, 1995) and others have called standpoint theory—a consideration of the social construction of knowledge with particular regard for its consequences for those not traditionally seen at the empowered centers of social groups.

Difference and Diversity

Difference and diversity dichotomize individuals and groups into self and other, us and them. As homogeneous as a group may appear from either an insider or outsider position, there will be distinctions that matter. Some types of individual distinctiveness are valued within a particular group, whereas other manifestations of distinctiveness are abhorred by the group. When individual or subgroup distinctiveness is labeled as *difference*, it is often stigmatized. It may be seen as needing adjustment, enhancement, or alteration in order to be assimilated into community, for example, by substitution of oral language for signed language (Goffman, 1963a; Robertson, 1995). Only what is perceived to be relatively innocuous or beneficial to the whole group or to the most powerful insiders will be willingly accepted. What is perceived to be too strange or dangerous may be met with systematic attempts at eradication. Distinctiveness that becomes labeled as *diversity* within community is generally more positively thought of as enriching, interesting, or rejuvenating. Although theoretically, differences and diversity within community can be politically neutral, they can also cause or reveal tensions. As with difference, too much diversity within a group may create complications—especially regarding individual rights and communal responsibilities. The always present tension between common good and individual rights can become more obvious or troublesome (Frazer & Lacey, 1993; Knight-Abowitz, 1997). At times, these complications may be met with displeasure or hostility, but at other times such complications may be seen as welcome opportunities for change (Balin, 1994; Boyd, 1996). Although they can be disruptive and disorienting, internal difference and diversity seem to be necessary to distinguish one insider from another within social groups, and will be invented if they are not discovered.

Because individuals within community are not perfectly alike in every aspect of their beings, accommodations necessarily arise that account for the diversity and differences among community members. The symbolic nature of community is what reconciles individuality and commonality (Cohen, 1985). Communities that proclaim the equality of all, claims Cohen, may mute expressions of difference yet still institutionalize ways of conferring differential status. These distinctions will be clear to insiders, although they may not be apparent to outsiders. What Minow (1990) calls the "dilemma of difference" hinges on the response to the related questions of whether to highlight or ignore differences in the service of social justice and equality.

Mead (1934) offers additional insight on the relation of self and group identity, with particular emphasis on the development of symbolic representation of shared meanings. The internalizations of shared meanings, the roles of the other members of one's community, and the larger, more generalized meanings of the group as a whole are developed as the individual matures as a member of the community. This internalization of the generalized other is demanded of the members of a society as necessary for its functioning. This self in relation to others is constructed in meaningful contexts through specific practices and social relations. Practices become routinized and institutionalized as roles. Role identity—for example, as a decision-making teacher or as a competent ninth grader—offers secure grounding for this developing sense of self.

Sense of Community

Opportunities to acknowledge social connections and identities within community are available during formal ceremonies or everyday practices. Sometimes ceremonies are designed to bring invited outsiders or newcomers into community with those in the group, bid farewell to those who are leaving, or mark changes in internal status. They also evoke a sense of being in community across the membership.

A sense of community may be demonstrated by members' feelings and practices that indicate interconnectedness, interdependency, and a commitment to the group and all its members. The term *sense of community* is often used to describe the participants' recognition of this interconnectedness, as well as to describe the interconnectedness itself. It is not necessary to feel a sense of community in order to act as if one is in community, but a sense of community generally is felt at least some of the time by community members and is considered a reliable indicator that community is present. In addition, although an outsider can observe that insiders feel a sense of community with each other, this sense of community does not transcend the borders of the group. Outsiders do not experience a sense of community.

Mijuskovic (1992) writes that the desire to overcome loneliness serves as a basic motivational drive for human beings, prompting people to form communal relations that evoke feelings of connectedness. Because the complexities of societal organization reconfigure what might once have been communal bonds into contractual ones, the sense of being in community can become lost, bringing about a sense of loneliness and alienation. In order to support the sense of belonging that alleviates such loneliness, occasions that mark or evoke a sense of being in community must occur regularly. Such occasions may also be manufactured or improvised when conditions indicate that they are needed, especially during crises or soon after they occur.

As Mews (1971) reminds us, conflict, discord, inequity, and so on, exist within social groups. Members may be bound together in mutual interdependence, but the fact of such interdependence is no guarantee that members will love each other, or that one member will not benefit unfairly at the expense of another. Sacrifice for the sake of others may not be rendered willingly. The interdependent social relations may exist but may not engender the related feelings of love, respect, or commitment that are elements of a sense of community. Following this observation, Mews points out that a social group can exist for some time without its members' feeling a sense of community, and can go for most, if not all, of its existence without any of its members' developing what he calls communion.

Communion is a "cognitive recognition of feeling," an acknowledged awareness of certain social relations and the emotions they evoke, such as love or respect. Like a sense of community, communion is a state of being in relationship that creates the very bonds it acknowledges. This means, for example, that the bonds of communion, marked by deep feelings of connection, flower as conscious recognition of the connections and the emotions they engender. The experience of communion is marked by an intensity and sense of totality greater than that engendered by a sense of community. But the difference between the two states is not merely one of degree. The state of being in communion can occur even when the actors are not co-members within a particular social group. Communion can exist, then, within or outside a community.

Moments of communion can be deliberately evoked during the times when a community joyfully celebrates itself or heartbrokenly mourns its losses: a Mass, a graduation ceremony, a memorial service. Moments of communion can also occur during what Csikszentmihalyi (1995) calls "flow"—intense experiences of "egolessness, merged action and awareness, high concentration, clear feedback, control, and enjoyment of the activity for its own sake" (p. 138). Intense moments of communion can also result when the community or a subgroup within it feels threatened or otherwise unusually beset by stresses, or when groups band together to achieve a superordinate goal that is to their mutual benefit (Mead, 1934; Sherif, Harvey, White, Hood, & Sherif, 1988).

Mews (1971) writes that "It is the fate of communions always to be transformed into societal or communal structures. Communion is unstable, fleeting, emotional. It is difficult to maintain over time" (p. 30). Because communion momentarily suspends but does not eliminate or tolerate diversity or individual interests, it creates a union that cannot sustain itself indefinitely. The intrinsic tensions of human interrelationship creep back into significance.

Also, because communion artificially suspends difference, moments of communion rarely include all members of a community. Therefore, the intensity of communion can threaten a community when such unions form within. Communities seek to normalize and institutionalize moments of communion into communal or societal institutions or organizations. Because it generally is in the interests of a community to continue its own existence rather than to dissolve, the co-opting of moments of communion—turning them into normative customs, celebratory rituals, or honored institutions—can reduce their fragmenting risk and increase the likelihood that they will strengthen stable communal relationships.

Community of Practice

Although all human beings are thought to have an innate need for affiliation (Maslow, 1962), the ways available to establish the affiliations associated with community are locally specific. One learns how to be in community as one engages in social relations with others. One learns that some social relations, in particular contexts, are not those of community. Similarly, one learns that some social relations and contexts bring about feelings of being in community within one group but not another. In consequence, learning how to be a competent community member can take quite some time and may require intensive monitoring of the less competent by those more competent. This is particularly evident in what are called communities of practice.

A community of practice is one within which there are unequal levels of power and knowledge, sustained by a system of learning that ensures, over time, the continuation of the existence of the community (Lave & Wenger, 1991; Minar & Greer, 1969; Sizer, 1992; Vanderslice & Farmer, 1994). The movement from apprentice to master within the community of practice is reflected in the novice's increasing self-identification of herself as a fully participating member of the community, as an expert practitioner. Schools are sites of communities of practice, and apprenticeship is the mode of learning that ensures their continuation. In schools, learning is a central practice of their memberships, as it is in all communities, but with an important difference. Although learning is one process through which the continuation of any community may be effected, in a community of scholars learning is considered to be the central practice as well as a process through which one acquires competence. Teachers instruct students directly and indirectly, and provide opportunities for students to increase their competence in reading, mathematics, and other academic pursuits. They also provide explicit and implicit facilitation of other practices, values, and beliefs necessary for full and expert participation in community. More experienced students provide additional examples of competence in the social relations of community for the novices or newcomers. Through successive approximations and extensive practicing, novices learn how to feel, think, and act competently with regard to the norms of practice within the group.

Professional community is a term used to describe some communities of practice. Professional communities, in addition to "the practice" and system of apprenticeship, also have a base of clients for whom they practice. Despite the inherent difficulties that make such a community complicated to establish and sustain, the presence of a professional community of educators is of great importance to the reformation and restructuring of urban schools (Dorman, 1987; Lipsitz, 1984; Louis & Kruse, 1995; National Middle School Association, 1982; Oakes et al., 1993; Staessens, 1991). The development and strengthening of shared norms and values are seen as the bedrock without which other elements of professional community will falter.

THE RESEARCH CASES

The research sites are a private Catholic elementary school (St. Margaret's Academy Elementary School), an all-girls private Catholic high school (St. Margaret's Academy High School), a remedial writing class in an urban college, and a restructured public middle school (Uptown School). In three cases, my presence in the schools was due to my participation in funded multiyear research projects. The fourth site, the remedial writing class offered by the urban university, was not part of a larger project. Although none of the research projects was designed specifically to examine the notion of community, at every site the participants expressed and demonstrated that the idea of community was very important to them. The local notions of community, in every case, played a significant role in the findings of each project.

In each research project, I functioned as a participant-observer, although the emphasis on participation or observation varied significantly from setting to setting. Only in Uptown School did I participate in the daily life of the school as an agent of change rather than as a disinterested observer. During the 3 years I spent at Uptown, I worked with staff, students, and parents on various projects and taught a qualitative research class to students. At every site I collected data in the form of field notes and analytic memos, audio- and videotapes, interviews, and documents. In addition to my university colleagues, the Uptown students and staff and the writing class tutor have been particularly helpful in shaping and critiquing my understandings of the data collected.

The two multiyear projects roughly overlapped, the Uptown work beginning 4 months earlier and ending 4 months later than the work in the two Catholic schools. The concurrence of the two projects was felicitous to this proposed research for a significant reason: Despite the differences between the schools, and between the research philosophies and goals underpinning each project, the notion of community emerged clearly as one that was extremely important to the participants at each site. The tracing of the mutual influences one project had upon the other did not deny or confirm "contamination" of design or findings but rather demonstrated how constant comparison between the two enriched the inquiry in both.

I listened to what the participants told and showed me about what was important about community, then examined how these were related to the practices that meant community to the participants. I made an important presumption for the purpose of this work, that is, that people did not deliberately misrepresent their beliefs in the words and other practices that I examined. This is not to say that every possible nuance of meaning was intelligible to any of the participants, including me, and most particularly not to say that I have any more accurate knowledge of the consonance of their words, practices, and beliefs than they do themselves. For example, being good and appropriate at St. Margaret's were gendered practices as well as community work when viewed from an outsider perspective. The insiders did not consider this observation particularly significant.

As Conway (1985) writes, people develop interrelated systems of beliefs and disbeliefs that they use to construct meaning, and these belief sets may well differ from group to group within a society. Practices or events that look the same across sites from an outsider perspective are not necessarily understood similarly by the insiders. Superficially dissimilar practices may closely parallel each other in at least some of their multiple meanings. The same words may convey different meanings. Different beliefs may be expressed with similar words or actions from site to site or from moment to moment in any one site.

In each site, community emerged as an important construct for the participants, although its meanings and practices differed from site to site. Vulnerability, fragility, and resilience differed as well. In order to better understand the notion of community within and across the sites, I sought to document and understand answers to the following open-ended questions: What do people say and believe about community? What do they *do*? That is, what practices are understood to evoke community regardless of their latent or manifest functions, and which are not? How do their words, beliefs, and practices together engender or fail to engender the social relationships and feelings about these that are recognized as community by those within the group? What emerges as consistently important, and what seems to be of only local importance, with regard to notions of community? I considered the evidence in light of what I have earlier outlined as necessary elements for the existence of community. This process made it possible to identify moments of vulnerability, fragility, and resilience specific to each group.

St. Margaret's Academy Elementary School

The Catholic schools were two of the sites visited during a 2-year research project (Richard Blot, principal investigator) funded by the Facilitator Center of the State of New York that undertook to examine the social construction of success in Catholic and public schools (Blot & Calderwood, 1995). I was the investigator at these two schools, which I will call St. Margaret's Academy Elementary and High Schools. (All sites and participants are designated by pseudonyms.) Although I spent time in all grades of the elementary school, my focus in the high school was on the first months of ninth grade only.

In the academic year 1993–94, 74% of the 173 enrolled students at St. Margaret's Academy Elementary School were girls. Most of the 36 boys were clustered in pre-K through first grade. There was some economic diversity among the families whose children were enrolled at the school, although the tuition (almost $3,000 per child per year) precluded the enrollment of working-class or poor students. The school was proud of its ethnic and racial diversity as well as the fact that it admitted many non-Catholic students. Whatever the religious affiliation of the student, he or she was expected to participate in and receive a grade for religion class. Every student was required to attend the monthly Mass, and all students were expected to join in the prayers during morning meeting, before lunch, and at dismissal. There was a faculty of 15. St. Margaret's Academy Elementary School was an institution within a functional community, more specifically, a spiritual community.

St. Margaret's Academy High School

In 1994, St. Margaret's Academy High School had a student population of 426 girls. One hundred and fourteen were ninth graders. Nearly all of the students and staff were Catholic. There was a staff of 38, all White, four of them men. Thirteen Sisters were on staff. Fifteen of the total staff taught ninth graders. Like the elementary school, the high school was also an institution within a functional, spiritual community.

The academic curriculum at St. Margaret's was configured similarly to those examined by Bryk et al. (1993) and cited by a number of other studies (Coleman & Hoffer, 1987, e.g.) as typical of Catholic secondary schools. St. Margaret's was considered a college preparatory school, a subcategory of schools that are rigorous in the academic expectations for all students. The principal of the school described it as far more academically demanding than the local public schools, and more academically demanding than most of the other Catholic high schools for girls in the area. According to presumed ability, students were assigned to classes designated honors, Regents, or non-Regents. All classes were considered to be preparatory for college.

Uptown School

The public middle school, Uptown School, was the site of a collaborative school–university research grant (Michelle Fine, primary investigator), funded by the Bruner Foundation, which is interested in promoting alternative evaluation studies in schools. One of the purposes of this project was to ascertain specific information about the work and effectiveness of the school. My initial task was loosely defined as documenter of the school culture. This research project was designed as participatory action research arising from the collaborative inquiry of students, staff, and parents.

Although many students attended the school because it was in their neighborhood, for the staff and for a significant number of students and parents, structurally, Uptown School was a values community.

In the 1993–94 academic year, Uptown had a staff of six full-time teachers, a director, a secretary, three part-time teachers, a part-time administrative assistant, and about 125 students. The director combined teaching and administrative duties. She had all the typical duties of a school principal, but technically she was under the authority of the building principal. The next year (1994–95), there were seven full-time teachers, three part-time teachers, three teaching interns, a student teacher, director, secretary, part-time administrative assistant, and 140 students. The seventh teacher, who held a special education degree, was hired because the school had added 12 students officially classified as MIS-1, a special education label for students who have mild disabilities. The school was a member of the Coalition of Essential Schools, an affiliation of public, private, and parochial schools that subscribe to nine essential principles, and many of the staff reported that its daily practices upheld the principles of the coalition (McQuillan & Muncie, 1994; Muncie & McQuillan, 1992, 1993; Sizer, 1992).

The Remedial Writing Class

The fourth instance was an independent, unfunded, single-semester research project overseen by Richard Blot. From late January to mid-May 1990, I was an invited participant-observer in an experimental remedial writing course offered to 15 specially selected undergraduates at one of the colleges of Urban U. About half the students were deaf, half were hearing. All but one of these students had previously failed a basic writing exam (the Writing Assessment Test, known as the WAT), which serves a gatekeeping function for admission to undergraduate matriculation at Urban U., and had taken at least two semesters of remedial writing courses. The WAT was a timed essay test given to students seeking matriculation at the college. The essays were read and graded by two examiners who rated them from 1 to 6, with 1 being a very poor score. The scores were added together, and a passing score was 8. The guidelines for grading the WAT were not hard and fast. The essay was expected to be coherent and well argued, and the form of the essay was expected to be conventional as to spelling, syntax, word agreement, and so on. Some of the students in this class had taken the WAT eight times and had failed it eight times. Their teacher, Sharon, and Margaret, a tutor for the deaf students, worked together as a teaching team throughout the semester. As we will see, this remedial writing class was a marginalized segment of an institution that retained vestiges of functional community. The class itself, however, fit the definition of neither a values nor a functional community.

A PREVIEW OF THE FOLLOWING CHAPTERS

The next three chapters are organized around the conditions that I believe must be present in order for the common practices of a group to become practices of community. This organization is necessarily loose because the conditions—creating group identity, accounting for internal difference and diversity, learning how to be in community, and celebrating community—are not separable one from the other. Sometimes, for example, celebrations construct meaningful differences as well as common identity. The process of learning how to be in community often includes the learning of new ways to label oneself, or to find oneself different from another.

The focus of Chapter 2 is to demonstrate elements of group-identity-building at the four research sites, as told or demonstrated to me by the participants at each site. Chapter 3 examines how the four groups make internal difference and diversity significant or insignificant. For each group, the entwining of internal and external differentiation is important and unique. In Chapter 4, I examine several examples of how the practices of community are learned by the participants of all four groups. The chapter also includes some examples of how communal social relations are celebrated. Chapters 2, 3, and 4 all examine instances of vulnerability, fragility, and resilience as they arise in relation to these foundational elements of community. Chapter 5 is devoted to a summative comparison of the nature and function of the above elements of community for each group. This lays the groundwork for consideration of the implications for building and sustaining resilient community in schools and other groups.

CHAPTER 2

Identity in Community

The importance of the borders and boundaries that mark community identity varied for the groups I studied. As we will see, the remedial writing class constructed the most tenuous of boundaries, bolstered by highly politicized and threatening borders. The three schools, in contrast, constructed borders that were much less dangerous.

Considerations of justice and moral community, as laid out in Chapter 1, held different significance for the groups in this study as they marked out their group identities. For some, these issues were situated in struggle. For others, considerations of justice did not trouble their considerations of whom to include and exclude from community.

As stated earlier, community identity is constructed in the ordinary practices of group members. At each site, people have shown me, through their words and activities, what they believe and do not believe about themselves as being in or not being in community. They have clearly marked out the boundaries and borders of community through their decisions about inclusion and exclusion. Their words and activities make the identities they have constructed vibrantly visible. We can learn much from them about the important work of creating identity in community.

A COMMUNITY OF WRITERS

An important element of constructing the boundaries of community is accomplished in the coalescence of a collective identity that sets the group apart from other groups. This was an especially poignant process for the remedial writing class at Urban U. The class had been formed because the university had designated a common identity for the students as failing writers in need of remediation, based upon their continued failing of the Writing Assessment test. The group identity in the remedial writing class that struggled to emerge was based upon the students' and teachers' recognition of the commonality the students shared as struggling writers gaining competence (Calderwood, in press-b).

Because these writers had been stigmatized by the college as linguistically incompetent, a politicized border surrounded them. This stigma had consequences beyond those associated with a disparaged self-image or group identity. The WAT exemplified both the power to stigmatize and the stigma itself.

24

The students who could not successfully cross the border fiercely guarded by the scorers of the WAT would continue to be denied matriculation. The event of preparing for and taking the WAT was an act of attempted border crossing that would be successfully completed by just two students that semester.

If the group could transform their collective identity into one that they could honor, the border that the WAT represented would lose much of its power. The WAT might still determine matriculation, but it might no longer have the power to demolish the students' sense of worth and self-respect.

The teachers, Sharon and Margaret, strove to support the students' attempts to overcome their internalized acceptance of their stigmatized identities and their associated sense of helplessness and despair about their academic competence and progress. They deliberately set about to encourage the students to find strength and dignity in their commonalities. Sharon, for example, called the group a community of writers during every class, and she and Margaret frequently stressed the importance of writing as a social process.

The students, too, participated in the work of building a creditable common identity for themselves. This was accomplished most frequently in oral, signed, and written conversation. Let us turn to one written conversation, conducted on an interactive computer network, in order to learn how they built the connections that support a sense of commonality.

Getting to Know Each Other

During the remedial writing class's first interactive computer conversation session, the students spent just under an hour chatting with each other on the computer network. This was the third class meeting and they were still getting to know each other. They were friendly, funny, and, most of all, candid. The following are selections from that conversation:

Vanessa: I am so happy to meet everyone that is in this class. this class is alright Nelson.

Anna: well ernesto and im curious what you doing after this class? and are you hanging out or what?????

Sylvia: Hello everybody. I am happy to be here AGAIN! But hoping to pass the w.a.t.

Mai: Marcia, yes, I talk too much, but your voice is low because we can't hear from u, ha!

Nelson: NO I AINT GO NOWHERE ERNESTO, U GOT TO BE PATIENT CUZ YOU NEED TO PASS THE WAT IN ORDER FOR YOU TO FORGET ABOUT THIS CLASS.

Nelson: SO, WHAT DO U THINK OF DEAF PEOPLE TODAY IN UR COLLEGE LIFE?

Nelson: DO U THINK THAT DEAF PEOPLE ARE THE SAME AS OTHER DEAF PEOPLE LIKE ME FOR EXAMPLE?

Sylvia: Nelson, I think DEAF people are just like me or anyone else. I've learn a lot throughout the years, one thing that I have learn is "not to hate or discriminate someone because they are handicapped or because of the color of their skin?

Alicia: Nelson, at one time I never thought of deaf people as being dumb, instead that they couldn't hear.

Marcia: Alicia, i have been depressing since i was student at ( ) college in fall 88. i was so upset and ashamed to show anyone about my writing skills. but later on i realized that no one had a perfect writing skills and that make me feel good and you should be.

James: ALICIA, THATS TRUE ABOUT ACADEMIC WRITING BEING DEPRESSING BUT JUST HANG IN THERE AND YOU WILL MAKE IT THROUGH

Sylvia: Nelson I am sorry it took me so long to answer your question but I was answering other people also. Anyway I think that if I was to go deaf or be deaf I would at first feel bad and very sad. I know I would cry, the reason why I say all this is because I am a very sentimental person and because I have never experience anything like deafness. I have experience blindness but not deafness.

Denise: It is my sixth took wat. Wondering if my behind will sit on the chair forever

Tom: Denise I'm not worried about your behind I'm worried about your poor frustrated readers of the WAT you will pour all your frustration so well into the next WAT their ears and eyes will burn.

The intimate revelations of struggle, the fear of the WAT, and an emerging sense of shared identity as struggling writers began early in the semester. Even the interpreter, Tom, couldn't resist offering his good-humored support to the establishment of a sense of community among the struggling writers. His comment sets up the WAT as the enemy, not only of Denise but of the whole group. They had a common history of failing this gatekeeping exam. The most visible difference among the group members—being hearing or deaf—was being neutralized and used to underscore the more important commonality—the need to pass the WAT.

Establishing the Struggle

As we will notice in the St. Margaret's Academy Elementary School example also, significant differences among members of the writing class were effectively neutered and transformed into the glue of commonality. However, unlike what happened at St. Margaret's, these differences were not treated as if they had been extinguished but were used over and over again to set up and underscore the students' belief that their common identity as members in a community of writers was far more salient than their many differences. Another conversation, this time face to face, shows how this work continued.

Sharon: Okay, let's hear some of your comments about this approach to reading and writing, cause it's fairly new for you, isn't it? Okay, you tell me what your reactions, what you've learned, or what you didn't . . .
Enrique: I guess the reading, and us writing, is the struggle that we started when we came here and took the first WAT. Then we were nervous about it, and it was just seeing, the struggle, what was best to do. But now, we took the second test and began, we struggled again, we tried our best and we struggling, struggling again. But this time this struggle is making us seem like the WAT is nothing. We can relax and think how easy the test will be by just struggling now.
Sharon: Are you just saying that? You're saying we. How do you feel personally? I mean, by your reading an autobiography and having questions that you have to back on and re-read and think about things, and then write directly to the text. Very complicated.
Enrique: Yeah, it is.
Sharon: What does it do for you? Don't think about the WAT!

Enrique's statement encapsulated an aspect of group identity—that of struggling writers. Sharon, while giving Enrique an opportunity to retract or otherwise amend this statement, reinforced the incorporation of this desirable group identity by stressing the work that they all needed to do. She implied that what was good for the group sense of community was also good for the individuated sense of self, thus promulgating particular attitudes and beliefs. Later in the conversation:

Sharon: So that's great, what you're saying, that if you really sort of hold on to that, that no one, WAT or anything else, can tell you, that you don't understand. That's what I'm saying. If you get it out of your heads that this WAT is really an indication of something about you. Then you begin to move on to what is important in learning to read and write. It's not simply the reading and writing, as Enrique said. It's the interaction, and all the other things that happen when you write. The experiencing of, you know, the word and all those things.
Margaret: And related to your experience, your world, make connections.
Sharon: That's what every great writer and reader does, right? You try when you pick up something. And let's face it. So often, many text-

books leave us out, the majority of us. That's why they're so difficult. We're not there, there's nothing to relate to. These are foreign words, right, that almost on purpose say "Stay away from me." Right? And this is a problem. But this is one of our battles, right? Many of us in this room belong to groups of people who have silenced voices, right? Not silent, but silenced, you know, for many economic or social or educational reasons. You have to find your own voice. And that's what you have to do, right? But you have to understand that the WAT is a device for measuring something very coldly. Right! How many errors you make in "s" or "ed". But it does not in any way measure what happens here, or here, (indicating her head and her heart) when you pick up a book or when you begin to write. If you really can begin to see for the first time in your lives that reading and writing, you know, sort of come together, pull each other, right? Then you've come further than a lot of people I've taught in seventeen years.

Margaret: Who have passed the WAT.

Sharon and Margaret revealed their objectives to the class quite explicitly. The class had much in common. Their common struggle not only presented an opportunity to feel a sense of community but also drew a boundary between them and those who had passed the WAT. Their "stigma" became inverted into a badge of honor—one that set them apart yet again from those who were outside this group (Cohen, 1985; Goffman, 1963a).

They intended for the students to disregard the WAT as a legitimate measure of assessment, for, as Sharon said, it could reveal nothing about them as readers and writers. She likened the WAT to the textbooks many had encountered that seemed engineered to ostracize people of color, users of nondominant varieties of English, or users of another language entirely. The WAT, too, handicapped those with linguistic differences, for there were no allowances made for the influence of dialect or first language, despite legal precedence which indicated that these should be taken into account (Labov, 1982).

The teachers wished the students to develop as readers and writers who could read not only the word but the world (Freire & Macedo, 1987). This Freirean framing of literacy was a frequent and explicit message stated by Sharon and Margaret to the students. Learning to think of themselves as being in community was sometimes a task consciously undertaken, sometimes one that was accomplished in the pursuit of some other task.

Noticing Commonality

Sometimes, in order to forge the sense of commonality that would construct community boundaries, real differences—borders, such as those of color, gender, or linguistics—needed to be neutralized. The implications of linguistic differences were discussed in the conversation on March 20. Margaret said,

> I was asked to talk about this course not too long ago. And that's one of the things that I said. I was comparing the deaf students to the hearing students and I said, "You know, there aren't a lot of differences. There are more similarities than there are differences. There are similar struggles." And, I think, that's something important that I've learned this course. There are so many similarities and people tend to focus on the difference. The woman I was talking to wanted to know all the differences. And I couldn't come up with any.

Margaret was well aware of the great diversity among the group members. But she was saying that their differences paled in significance when the much more important commonality was considered. She explicitly laid out the proposal of celebrating similarity without denying difference. Sharon built upon Margaret's words:

> Well, obviously, there's a lot of assumption there. If you have a class and you tell people half are people who are hearing and the other half are people who are deaf or have hearing impairments, people come with these assumptions, right. And I know what they are assuming about all of us, right? That word handicapped that I hate, that we all hate. They figure that in some way we're all handicapped, me included. You realize that. I'm involved with it. If I'm your teacher, then they look at me, as, "How can somebody with all that education be doing that? What's wrong with her?" Right? I ask myself sometimes, too, to be honest. And as Margaret said, we all have great similarities. But I wanna say that I think differences are important. That we should honor our differences. That's the problem. That's when we've been hung up about stuff on the WAT. Because we're different. Because we're deaf, or we're hearing impaired, or we speak English as a second language, or English as a second dialect. Or this, or this, or that. We're made to feel as though we don't have the right. I mean, you have to honor your differences. Look what Helen Keller did, look what Malcolm X did. They honored their differences. They grew to learn that in order to feel respect for themselves, they had to honor that they were different, right. That it is not anything to be ashamed of, right? It's something to honor. How many people in this country can speak another language or three languages? The whole world can, except most Americans. We lose our perspective.

Transforming Stigma

Sharon reiterated that everyone in the group, herself included, had been stigmatized by outsiders. She continued the work of inverting that stigmatization into honor. This was a moment of important border work being done—
asserting, from an insider perspective, a reordering of the power to stigmatize
or honor. Now the outsiders were stigmatized—they lacked an important attribute held by the members of this group. The WAT, similarly, could con-
ceivably be divested of its power to stigmatize or to call attention to stigmata.

If the students were to honor their differences, as Sharon urged them to
do during that conversation, they needed to be able to reconcile their own
affirmation of their differences with the derogation reflected by those who used
the dominant variety of written English to judge their academic performance.
But ultimately, they were not able to accomplish this. Here, then, lies the basic
contradiction that undermined the success of the pedagogy. The students were
expected by the university, by their teachers, and by themselves to fail the test;
they had always failed the test. Being encouraged to disavow the WAT's le-
gitimacy could not lessen its power to marginalize. Although the students
offered statements of resolve and determination to overcome their fear of the
next WAT, and professed an understanding of the relationship between reflective reading and writing that would foster their literacy competence, it was
not certain that they were speaking what they truly believed. How deeply had
they internalized the message that they were as inferior as their performance
would be judged?

The construction of community identity was an important endeavor for
this group of struggling writers. It involved the difficult tasks of diminishment
of the importance of intragroup diversity and difference, the assertion of the
primary elements of their common struggle, and the inversion of stigma into
honor. Significantly, however, the work of transforming stigma into honor
did not directly impact upon the practice of writing, ostensibly the central and
identifying practice of a "community of writers." Unfortunately, the emphasis on reading and writing autobiographies was effective to only a limited degree in improving the writing skills of the students, because they did very little
writing and spent little time critically examining their own writing. The main
benefits of using autobiography as subject were to foster self-reflection and
strengthen a sense of community during their discussions revolving around
the theme of struggle, as considered by Enrique:

> All right. It taught me a lot. It taught me too, the part that seemed her
> experience also seemed my experience, you know? I mean, struggling
> you know. I've struggled, I read and I have to do the papers. Now I
> get sick, but I still gotta do the papers. Understand, that's a struggle,

too! Understand? And I was in the hospital, and I was like, "Oh, God, where this lady's at?" But I still gotta read the book. [Laughter]

Longing to Escape the Struggle

The students were willing to continue their struggles with literacy because, as Bourdieu (1984) elaborates, they all longed to reposition themselves in the social system through the acquisition of educational capital, as passages from their writing exams testify:

> School is important also, because you need a good education to get a good job and a good life. If you should have a stable job that pays good salary, then you can maintain a loving family. You will be able to buy a house, a car and make your family comfortable.

> When you have your education and career, then life will be better.

> Young people could have a good career and good salary with diploma or degree. It's important to have a good salary so they could afford a place to stay, pay debits, buy clothes and food to keep them a good healthy. Without the degree, it's impossible to get a job that had a good salary. . . .

Interestingly, the stake that the students had in acquiring educational capital was based on a deep desire to disassociate themselves from the very stigmatizations that the teachers set up as marks of honor and dignity. They longed to leave the struggle and the stigma behind. Assimilation into the larger college community was a goal for the students, but one not likely to be achievable as a group. The normative pull of larger campus community was in part structured upon the exclusion of marginalized groups such as this class (Ginsberg, 1994; Magolda & Knight-Abowitz, 1997; Opotow, 1990; Smiley, 1992). A few individuals might slip out of marginalized status, but only in tandem with the continuation of the marginalization of those who needed remediation. Their success necessitated a betrayal of their fellow struggling writers. The teachers' continued insistence upon the critical examination and inversion of their stigmatized and marginalized status kept the wounds of their marginalization raw and oozing, with little hope of healing. The vulnerability of community for this group would coalesce around this wound. Attending to the vulnerability necessitated the maintenance of the painful and degrading stigma and marginalization of the students. The hope of building resilience from this vulnerability rested upon the other practices of the group, specifically writing.

Resisting Common Identity

On the part of some students, there was a deeply ingrained resistance to complete assimilation into group identity that deserves mention. The deaf and
hard-of-hearing students had feelings, such as pride or shame, about how
they used any ability to hear that they might have had. These feelings were
bound with a highly politicized sense of identity as being either in or out of
deaf culture. Having hard-of-hearing or hearing-impaired status seemed not
entirely determined by the amount of hearing ability an individual had but
was marked also by the use of lip reading and oral language. The hard-of-
hearing students wore hearing aids, but then so did Keith, who is deaf. Two
hard-of-hearing students did not use sign language at all and professed not
to understand it. They, along with the hearing students and me, had to learn
how to attend politely to the deaf students' conversation without looking at
the interpreter. The hard-of-hearing students did not consider themselves
part of the larger deaf community of which the deaf students were members. They were more isolated from each other and from campus activities
than were the deaf students, who maintained classroom friendships outside
the class. They seldom talked to anyone in the class other than Sharon or
Margaret, the teachers.

Nelson, a deaf man, spoke understandable English and Spanish and signed
in PSL (Pidgin Sign Language). His self-identification vacillated between deaf
and hard of hearing. Nelson remained aloof and somewhat isolated from the
other students. His signing was at issue. The deaf students regarded his Pidgin signs as evidence of his rejection of deaf culture. He usually spoke English
during class, as the deaf students preferred the interpreter's signing to Nelson's.
Marcia, another deaf student who had only recently learned to sign, usually
spoke for the same reason; the other deaf students were adamant about their
preference for the interpreter's signing, which was more standardized and
consistent than that of either Nelson or Marcia.

Nelson in particular maintained a separateness from the other students
that precluded his full acceptance of the group identity. He had spent much
of his life in relative isolation, which I learned through both observation and
conversation. He was a mainstreamed student all his academic life and had
not gone to elementary school with other deaf children. Consequently, he
learned English and Spanish as his first and second languages and considered
himself fluent in both. He learned his Pidgin signs in high school and had some
ability in American Sign Language (ASL), although the deaf students did not
consider him fluent at all. He believed that his education was superior to that
of the other deaf students, and that he himself was not handicapped by either
his lack of hearing or his education to the same degree as the deaf students.
Interestingly, he referred to himself sometimes as deaf and sometimes as hard

of hearing. His self-designation was deaf when he wanted me to know how difficult his life was and hard of hearing when he wanted to assert that he was better than the other deaf students. He did not ever compare or align himself with the hearing students to me in private conversation or in any class discussions.

The antipathy that deaf and hard-of-hearing students felt for each other was difficult to overcome because of its genesis in significant political and cultural standpoints that were essential to the personal and group identities of the students outside class (Deutch, 1990; Fine, 1990; Gans, 1992; Ginsberg, 1994; Opotow, 1990; Smiley, 1992; Wolfe, 1992). The tenacity of that particular antipathy within the group was a persistent vulnerability that could draw the students closer together or push them apart. Respecting and thus maintaining the important distinctions between deaf and hard-of-hearing status was insisted upon by some of the students and became an issue of contention. The way the contention was handled, as we see later, however, brought about an opportunity for the students to overcome, at least during class meetings, their active resistance to neutralizing this difference.

COMMUNITY AT UPTOWN IS A MATTER OF PERSPECTIVE

The work of building identity through the establishment and maintenance of boundary and border was also undertaken at Uptown school. This was accomplished in ways quite different from those utilized in the remedial writing class. This group's collective identity did not include the important element of stigmatized, failing, or struggling writer, for example, so it was less urgent to make the differences between insider and outsider identity significant. The students and staff at Uptown spoke and wrote much about the social relations within the group that marked them as being in or out of community.

What follows is a brief analysis of the responses to open-ended questions printed on the surveys distributed to staff, students, and parents at Uptown in fall 1992, 1993, and 1994 and in spring 1993 and 1994. The responses indicate what they believed supported or threatened community there. These comments also establish an idealized notion of what community should be like.

Uptown Staff Perspectives

The experience and support of a sense of being in community were particularly important to the staff. When the following were present, they were perceived by the staff to integrate the ideal vision of community at Uptown with its observable presence:

A basic agreement on a mission and a common vision

A sense of community

The necessity for specific events to celebrate community autonomy in
  developing curriculum

Having a voice

Being connected to students and staff members

Voluntary membership

Effective leadership

Feeling supported, included, valued, and respected

One person wrote that although dissent might impede the smooth functioning of a community, it was probably normal. Another believed that uncertain boundaries, secrets, and pockets of internal inclusion and exclusion
marked the group as surely as did its commitment to educating the students.
Others commented that membership and inclusion in a community were a
matter of choice on the part of the individual. The idea of an ideal community, as opposed to a real one, was often repeated—as was the notion that
community is a process.

As part of a combined confirmation check and information feedback regarding a study of staff decision-making (Calderwood, in press-a), I asked the
staff to respond in writing to several statements and questions about the school.
I learned that assumptions about shared values and beliefs, mission, desired
practices, and so on, supported the staff's beliefs that they were in community. Teachers wrote that they believed that:

> Teaching kids is one of the most important jobs in the world. That
> the school be as diverse as possible ethnically, racially, religiously,
> economically, and in ability. That we provide "equity" as far as
> possible (i.e., material provided at school for kids who do not have
> them at home.) That consensual decision-making is important to
> teach and live by. That all at Uptown, adults and kids, are both
> learners and teachers. That it is valuable the school is "a work in
> progress."

> We all believe that we're changing things, although there are different
> notions of what that is. We believe the public system has failed people.
> We all feel that we have input to a certain degree, although there are
> different levels. We believe we do good. We believe we provide value.
> We each think the others do good things for the school, are committed
> to kids, and work hard. We believe all this even though we know we
> have major differences.

The staff believed that it shared a strong commitment to the students in the school, and that this commitment withstood tensions or conflicts resulting from ideological difference. This commitment to the well-being of the students was a fundamental element of the individual and group identity of the teachers and one of the key referents of the school as a caring unit. It underscored the reality of internal difference and diversity within community as well. The Uptown community structure is that of a values community, where common beliefs and values have drawn together a more or less securely cohesive group, as a teacher's comment illustrates:

> I see Uptown as a work in progress with many aspects of a community: Students, teachers, and parents are stakeholders, to some extent there is a common vision which most can articulate. Ownership is felt by most to some degree. All have consciously chosen to be at Uptown.

The director told me, "One of the most mysterious things is what happens between what teachers teach and what kids learn." She said that the students had to teach her what they learned in class. One of the best ways to help people grow, she believed, was to have them reflect what they have learned as if they were teaching the material themselves, maybe offering one or two comments on what might be improved. She remembered that kids judge themselves harshly, that they are vulnerable and unsure. Because outside messages are about what they lack, she would rather speak about their potential than where they are now. She gave an example of a student who told her that he felt a responsibility to live up to the recommendation she had provided for him. She cited the 100 letters of support that helped ease another student's admission into high school. Every time he thinks about not doing his homework, he remembers those letters.

The director's example is telling—it highlights caring connections and accountability within community and indicates the attention lavished on individual students. It also shows that this director set the tone of professional identity as caring and sensitive educator. The overall community sense of identity, the boundary making, was built around this. Taken together, the staff and director's comments focused on the students' learning, and on themselves as facilitators of that learning. Connection, support, interdependence, being "all together," were important. One staff member explained the philosophy of teaching and learning at Uptown as follows:

> There is a view of teachers and students on a journey—teachers see themselves as learners. There are strong democratic values, strong advocacy of staff and students apparent in training. It is the opposite of

hand-feeding information to young minds. It is a joint venture centered on processes of change, growth, and learning. We're all together.

Uptown Parent and Student Perspectives

Parents indicated approval for the academic climate at the school and perceived the staff as caring, kind, and trustworthy. As parents, they felt welcome, respected, and nurtured. Cooperation, diversity, and harmony, a sense of family, accessibility, inclusion, and respect, were hallmarks of community for the parents. Community was described as a work in progress.

At Uptown, students' perceptions of community were anchored in a sense of trust, respect, and connection. Threats to group community included fractures of mistrust, disrespect, and disconnection. We asked the students: Have your feelings about Uptown changed or stayed the same since you first came to the school? Why? How did you feel then? How do you feel now? Examples of student statements indicate that feelings, changed or not, were far more positive than negative:

> They have definitely changed. At first I used to be scared and shy but now as you can see I am kind of open. Before I felt alone but now I have so many friends.

> Yes, I felt trapped. I fell open.

This last comment, "Yes, I felt trapped. I fell open," eloquently captures the free-fall of trust and vulnerability inherent in the risk of choosing to be in community. Community calls for a "leap of faith" in oneself and in those with whom one would be in community.

There was a change over time in the student evaluations of their pride in the school and in how they viewed teacher–student relationships. The evaluations became less positive for all students, and more dramatically so for eighth graders as they prepared to move on to high school. An explanation for this phenomenon is supported by the interviews with the graduates of the school, who almost unanimously remembered their Uptown days fondly, especially in comparison with their high school experience. The testimony of the graduates suggests that Uptown students measured their lived experience at the school against an imagined ideal school while they were at Uptown. Once they had spent some time in high school, however, they then measured their Uptown experience in light of the new information they had accumulated about another type of school experience. Uptown, in retrospect, was seen as closer to their ideal school.

The Nature of Community at Uptown

Taken together, the responses of the staff, parents, and students set out some markers of perceived community in Uptown. The themes of inclusion and diversity, of feeling connected, respected, and valued, were common to all three groups. Taking care of its members was a hallmark of this community. There was some acknowledgment that conflict, theft, injustice, privilege, and exclusion existed, although these were cited as threats to Uptown community.

Community at Uptown was fragile and always in process. Idealized community was used as a referent to judge the practices of community here. A group identity of being in community was measured by its similarity to being in idealized community rather than by the strengths of its resistance to or distance from some actual outside group. Thus the enactment of certain social relations such as respect for and attention to the needs of individual students among teachers, students, and parents needed to occur for community to be perceived as present, and for a collective identity based on communal relations to emerge. If the necessary social relations lapsed, even momentarily, the identity of community at Uptown quivered and cracked. The struggle to support the desirable social relations made the evaluative aspect of community identity salient here. That is, when there were undesirable social relations in play, the students clearly, and the staff ambivalently, would judge that they could not possibly be in community and thus that they could not be a community. Because being in community was highly valued at Uptown, much work was done by the staff and students to maintain those social relations and related feelings that connected them together in community.

The nature of community at Uptown was also dependent on the way that staff and student roles were understood and carried out. As we see in Chapter 3, these roles necessitated making internal difference and diversity visible and of paramount importance. There were contradictions and some ambivalence surrounding the constructions of the functions of internal diversity and difference that bore implications for group identity as a cohesive, caring community. On the one hand, attending to and celebrating individual differences and diversity was a signature characteristic of the identity of the group. On the other, the work done to reduce the tensions arising from differences and diversities revealed vulnerabilities and strengths within community at Uptown.

At Uptown School any disjunctions between ideal community and actual social relations were seen as potentially fracturing vulnerabilities. In consequence, the group acted to bridge the breaches they discovered. The students and parents relied on the staff to do most of this work to protect and strengthen the practices of community here. The value that they placed on trust and respect cannot be overemphasized, nor can the disappointment and disillusion that resulted when trust and respect were perceived to be violated. Fissures and fractures resulting from such breaches were considered especially damaging to the resilience of community here. Potential fissures and fractures were assiduously avoided through selective attention to the vulnerabilities exposed by differences between idealized and actual practices of community.

ST. MARGARET'S ACADEMY ELEMENTARY SCHOOL IS FAMILY

Over the span of 1½ years, I endeavored to learn how they constructed success at St. Margaret's Academy Elementary School (Blot & Calderwood, 1995). As they told me about success, they talked to me and wrote about themselves as family. They described trust, dependence, caring, and togetherness. They celebrated themselves as children of God. In contrast to the people at Uptown and the remedial writing class, they seldom used the word *community* to describe themselves or their social relations, but it was clear that they made a strong association between success and the social relations described elsewhere as those of community. Perhaps this was because the fundamental foundation of the spiritual community of which they were part was well established and absolutely secure (Blot & Calderwood, 1995). They were less concerned with who they were as a group than with the particular ways they expressed their communal relationships.

Nevertheless, as they told me who they were, and as they went about their normal business, they constructed and revealed their group identity. Much of this work was accomplished along with the more visible work of teaching and learning, as was the case in the remedial writing class and at Uptown School, although much less time and effort were spent on this identity work at St. Margaret's and much more time devoted to academic pursuits. Much of what they told me about who they believed themselves to be was in the context of their consideration of themselves as successful students and teachers.

Education and learning, a tolerance for diversity, Christian values, mutual respect, peace and compassion, and development of the whole person were the central values of the school, as stated in the brochure put together by the teachers. The brochure stated that these values were supported through religious studies; academic enrichment; structure; routine; dress code; acceptance of all races and creeds on an equal basis; small class size; individual attention; encouraging spiritual growth; a nurturing and caring environment; fostering partnership among students, teachers, and parents; and accountability and responsibility on the part of all. Friendships and other caring relationships, said the students and faculty, also belong on this list, as does a sense of togetherness, family, and community.

Students Described St. Margaret's Academy Elementary School

Small group interviews with the seventh and eighth graders were conducted in June 1994. The students' responses to the question, "What are the most significant things you have learned or experienced during your years at St. Margaret's?" most frequently included a statement that they had learned the importance of respect, both self- and other-directed. They gave supporting reasons for why this was so important. Prominent among the reasons was the necessity to tolerate and appreciate the ethnic, religious, and personality diversity among the students. As we see in the next chapter, this tolerance of diversity, a self-defined characteristic of the group, was accomplished by rendering difference and diversity insignificant and nonthreatening. Internal difference and diversity became commonality at St. Margaret's Academy Elementary School. This transformation was undertaken and accomplished with goodwill and sincerity by the students and staff.

The difference that they believed set them apart from other school groups was that they were a small, close-knit family who loved and respected each other. Also, the girls said that they appreciated feeling respected by the teachers, and were severe in their disapproval of the times when they felt disrespected. Such times were not frequent but were experienced as momentous when they did occur. This resonated with the pervasive concerns for justice that students at Uptown also found to be so important to the process of community.

The girls stressed the importance of friendships, of caring and close relationships. These were treasured all the more because the girls had learned that friendships can change over time. Being kind, being nice, were important. The eighth graders also said that they had learned that appearances such as skin color, clothes, money, or where one lived influence how people treat each other. They had felt the stings of prejudice, said some. This was not right, they said. Everyone was equal.

When asked, "What do you believe is the mission of Catholic education? How do you think St. Margaret's accomplishes this mission?" the girls listed close attention, caring and trustworthy teachers, love, friendship, and respect, opening minds, providing morals and goals, encouragement, and individualized education. One student was of the opinion that there were no differences between Catholic and public education except for uniforms and religion class. Several students said that one purpose of Catholic schools was to make money. When making comparisons, the girls regarded the generic public school as "other."

As we can see, these goals resonated with the descriptions the Uptown students gave about community in their school. The constant comparison of what people told me at each of these schools supported my belief that they were speaking about practices of community in both places, even when the word community was not used.

The students consistently told me to "put in the real things" when I wrote about the school. When I asked what were "the real things," they listed:

The closeness
We respect other students
One big and happy family
Caring teachers
Acts of personal kindness
The education
The relationship between the students and the teachers
The school is "not all it's cracked up to be"
This is a different school for the students than for the teachers
Small isn't necessarily better
There should be a reality course
We've learned how to keep things under control
We work with each other

As in Uptown School, tensions between real and idealized community were evident. Small wasn't necessarily better in a school that was "not all it's cracked up to be."

In summary, both the seventh and eighth graders were positive about the school, although sometimes less than flattering. They valued respect. They loved their friends and cherished their close relationships. They were a family together. The seventh graders judged success by measuring happiness, accomplishment of goals, by "looking in" beyond surface appearances. Students' having wonderful futures reflected the success of a school.

One girl wrote, "I decide if people are successful by looking in the inside of people, not the outside." This comment is an example of how it is possible to make certain kinds of diversity or difference (gender, ethnicity, social class) relatively unimportant. In fact, the ethos that kindness, honor, and spirituality were the measure of a person's worth rendered other demarcations unnecessary and unworthy of consideration. This does not mean that St. Margaret's students or staff would not acknowledge ethnicity, gender, or social class as meaningful. However, they said that they looked elsewhere to make value judgments about people. This was another example of how they distinguished themselves from outsiders, or from those in other schools who made much of ethnic, gender, and social-class distinctions. An important belief that supported this attitude was that the students and teachers were not just like a family but rather they *were* a family. The myth of family was that there were personality and role differences among the members that overwhelmed, even "whited out," other possible differences such as social class, gender, or race.

Maintenance of the myth of family was necessary to hide the vulnerability to community that intolerance, racism, and other exclusionary practices would expose. Exposure of the myth of homogeneous and loving family as fictive could have potentially fractured community at St. Margaret's Elementary School. Exploring this vulnerability was not seen as a way to strengthen community.

Staff Talk About St. Margaret's Academy Elementary School

Thirteen of the fifteen faculty members of St. Margaret's were interviewed in May and June of 1994. The teachers described the social relations at their school in terms similar to those used at Uptown. As at Uptown, tension was evident, here expressed in the question of just how common were the fundamental values of the staff. As we see in the next chapter, the differences between the lived reality and the idealized vision of common beliefs and goals were downplayed in order to construct a cohesive group identity as a caring family.

When responding to the question, "How do you know when you or your students or this school are successful? What does St. Margaret's do to help ensure success in the areas to which you referred?" the teachers often spoke of students' achievements as indicators of their own success. That is, when students did their best, took risks, or when "the light bulb goes on," the teachers and the students were successful. Teachers relied on feedback from the students to know whether they were successful. One teacher gauged his success by measuring how close he came to his goals, including his goals for his students' achievement: doing his best, student enjoyment and enthusiasm, autonomous learning. Another teacher said measuring academic success was easy, but spiritual success was harder to judge. She said that cooperation between teachers was essential to make success happen in the school. The school was successful if people recommended it to others, if there was connection between home and school.

People spoke of the mission of the school in the following ways: to provide an environment that enables students, to allow students to question, to encourage the child to grow to his or her fullest academic and personal potential. This mission was impeded somewhat, because the school could not provide sufficient services to children in need of extraordinary resources such as special education, social services, and guidance counseling. At St. Margaret's there were "small groups of people knit together by mutual respect." Teachers told me to mention the individual attention given to each student, the rich ethnic and religious diversity, the open communication between students and staff, the dedication of the staff, the comfort of the workplace, the supportive principal, and the openness and freedom to teach their religious beliefs.

One teacher, a gentle woman generous with hugs, kind comments, and expressions of care, began a richly sensitive and thoughtful conversation:

Teacher: I definitely feel like those words: [nurturing, caring] were near the top in my three adjectives. I would definitely say those are important, key words here. And I don't say that just between teacher and student. I would even say it's very much, even between teacher to teacher. You know this year has been a little difficult for me personally. I find a real genuine care and concern. I often come in and there's like, a little note on my desk. One day I came in and there were flowers from one of the other teachers. Different teachers, just in sharing things with them, just being, you know, sort of at wit's end. It's raised my level of consciousness of how people feel, say about, you know, do things like that for me. That helps you. Keeps your spirits up.

Calderwood: Is that different from your experience in other schools?

Teacher: My only other real experience is in another Catholic school. In the school I taught in before coming here, I did feel that same connectedness. I think that's, I can't say it's unique to Catholic schools. I think a lot of it depends on faculty. This place has its own uniqueness in that way. I find there's very much, in this school, there are as many maybe if not more, ratio-wise, needy, academically needy, students here as I taught in the Bronx. I know that my mission, that I have work to do this summer in terms of being able to really meet the needs academically of my higher level, you know, gifted and talented type students, who really can go places and those who are academically challenged on the same level. Finding the time to work with them in the classroom.

Calderwood: Do you have to do that? Or is that just your mission? Is that expected of you?

Teacher: I hate this word [entitlement], but I'm going to have to use it for lack of something else. The parents pay money for their child to come here to be educated. I feel that a child should come to, and that's even for public school I feel that way, that the teachers are being paid a salary and the child should come there to learn. To be taught and to learn. Yet, on the other hand, I also feel that if a child has special needs that cannot be met within that classroom, that should also be addressed as well, which is a real difficulty here in the school. I often think that sometimes parents take their child out of a public school setting and put 'em in a smaller classroom to avoid the educational evaluation and their child being labeled. As a parent, I respect that, because sometimes it is a maturity thing that a child could work out. But then, a child could be here, and if they have needs that really cannot be met in this room that I'm not even trained or qualified to aid them with, I feel I'm really doing them a disservice. And that's hard. I feel, it's my obligation, that they come here to learn and that I try to meet their needs. I'm not saying personal, but academically.

Teacher: [About low pay] Sometimes that's the hard part. I know commitment-wise I believe in Catholic education. I do. I think that being able to work with the children on a level where you can talk about life values and stuff, and integrate that across the board, very much helps with the integration of life skills.

Calderwood: Is that the mission of Catholic education? Is there a particular type of education that's Catholic?

Teacher: That's as I see it. I'm comfortable with teaching that way, so that's what I do. I don't know if that's necessary. I don't know if every person is that way. It's not to say that my way is the right way. I'm sure that there are many children who pass through their experience with me and get absolutely nothing. I've become much more reflective. I like my classroom to have a certain atmosphere to it, comfortable, lots of laughing. Sometimes I measure, I don't know if I can measure the academics of it that way, but I definitely measure other things by that. The classroom climate, so to speak. Can they [the students] ever take ownership of it [learning] when they're unhappy here? So, I always have a very strong goal to develop classroom atmosphere. I don't think that anything ever can be learned in any other kind of atmosphere. I treat them a certain way, and I won't allow them to treat me or anyone else in any other way. I feel I wouldn't be able to do that in a public school. I talk a lot about God, how God wants us to be, about spirituality. To ask someone to be a good, kind human being, but why? I think that's why I feel that way about religion, about the integration. Here there's no parish. We have a multicultural diversity of religion as well here in this school. In my class of fourteen, I only have four Catholics. I invite them to share their things, their religion. My own children have grown up really respecting other faiths, and I invite that very much here. In the way I teach, too, I'm always open to divergent thinking. You know, is there another way we could look at that? I feel in a public school, I wouldn't be able to appeal on that level. Just asking them to be a nice human being for the sake of being nice. Children always want to know why. We search for that in our adult spirituality. It's hard to make those right choices all the time, and why. Being able to connect that spirituality to it, you know, that higher level, in terms of learning and all life experience—not to be able to do that in a public school—I don't know if I could. Even maybe that nurturing, caring comes from that whole, that religion, no I mean spirituality. I think this is true for many of the people who work here. Discipline comes in there. I see it more as self-discipline. Maybe I'm looking at the wrong word. Maybe it's more of an ability of conformity. Life requires you, for success, for you to conform to certain standards and live up to certain expectations. And, little things like uniforms, mindless, obsessive as it may appear, are maybe little ways of learning that life skill. Having to line up, staying in a straight quiet line, sometimes we have to do it to be considerate of other people. In Catholic school, as opposed to public school, there are a lot more rules you have to conform to. And maybe learning it from an early age, of having to commit and follow through, as opposed to more freedom, so to speak, that's allowed in a public school. Maybe that teaches that skill in a way that you don't even realize. . . . Maybe it's that the parents have chosen this school for a reason, and some of that value is carried through at home.

This interview underscored the meaning of education, the mission of teaching, the relation of discipline to success, and how success was measured at St. Margaret's Academy Elementary School. Education was seen as a commodity parents bought for their children, and to which students were entitled. The students and teachers had responsibilities and commitments to keep in order for education to happen: The teachers had to meet the academic needs of all the students; the students had to commit to learning. Success at teaching was measured in various ways: feedback, hugs, a comfortable classroom climate with much laughter, expressions of affection between student and teacher. Diversity was valued. A sense of spirituality gave meaning, and propelled the caring and nurturing that were its expression.

The teacher was clear that teaching and learning of academics was of paramount importance. She recognized that students have other needs as well, which were not necessarily being met at this school, although she did her best to meet them. If these needs were met, it was most likely done coincidentally through academic learning. She believed that this was a major difference between this school and a generalized public school, which she imagined to have a greater scope of resources available. Note, however, that this teacher drew on the same professional and personal resource—a commitment to doing her best to serve the needs of her students—drawn on by the Uptown and remedial writing class teachers.

Another boundary was set up—Catholic schools attended to spirituality, public schools didn't. The border was clearly drawn because she regarded spirituality as such a very superior reason to be a good human being. Another characteristic of her school, the insistence on conformity, has been found by social psychologists (Schwartz, 1994) to support an esteem for tradition and traditional ways of acting and believing. She believed public schools lacked this characteristic and set no value on it.

The principal of St. Margaret's Academy Elementary School compared the school to a family as she explained that the school was a community:

> Well, I think people can be themselves here. Our size and maybe our atmosphere encourage people to be themselves. And for whatever that's worth, sometimes we may, because of each individual feeling as though he or she could be himself or herself, sometimes we see idiosyncrasies. But, they might be hidden in a larger program, what- ever. I think if you feel as if you can be yourself, you're not busy about being something else. I think it has to do with the size and the atmo- sphere and the family unit. In a family most people can be themselves, that's where we are ourselves. I do think that it's not a totally correct comparison, but here there's a sort of a family atmosphere so that happens. Family is a difficult word. I don't know if it is the appropriate word, but it's a community, it's a place where people, where there's a bond. People care about each other.

Because they were family, people could be themselves. Differences be- came idiosyncrasies, individually situated and tolerable.

In summary, the staff described St. Margaret's Academy Elementary School as a nurturing, caring community that was successful at carrying out the mission stated in the school's self description: "Students are guided to- ward the development of their whole person so that ultimately they become aware that they have within themselves the resources to create a better world."

It was important for the students and staff of St. Margaret's Academy Elementary School to believe that they were a cohesive and tolerant family. The immediate social relations of nurturing, caring, and respect were impor- tant to their sense of themselves as in community. Their essential spiritual commonality was stressed. Not much consideration was given to the borders or boundaries of community here, other than a belief that they were not like public schools. The security of membership in an inviolate spiritual commu- nity reduced their need to attend to their borders and boundaries, for every human being was considered to be a member of this same spiritual family. They were generally comfortable in their self-identity as inclusive and tolerant of all, despite the visible presence of at least two exclusionary factors: economics and gender. Although enrollment in the school was ostensibly open to any student, the steep tuition and lack of scholarships precluded much economic diversity. The staff was predominantly female, itself an indicator of economic issues, White, and Catholic. Few boys attended the school, possibly a legacy of its previous history as an all-girls school. These factors did not seem to affect the predominant beliefs about their collective identity. Boys were welcome to enroll, for example. There was significant ethnic and religious diversity among the students, although, as we see in the next chapter, such diversity was treated as if it had little significance.

ST. MARGARET'S ACADEMY HIGH SCHOOL
LIVES THROUGH ITS PEOPLE

Many of the students were second-generation St. Margaret's students. Their mothers or other older relatives, including older sisters, were once students here. The intergenerational membership also marked the faculty. The principal and a number of teachers, including the dean of students and the dean of curriculum, were once students at the school. The mothers of the principal and the dean of students were former students. One social studies teacher was the mother of the gym teacher, who herself had been a student at the high school. One of the new teachers of religion and English was a fairly recent graduate of the high school, as was the biology student teacher. These two new staff members said that they balanced the slight awkwardness of the role change from students to teachers with the comforting feeling of coming home to teach. One woman said that St. Margaret's was a good place to start her teaching career. "People are helpful here, they are like a second family." St. Margaret's held a special place in her heart, she said. "Its spirit lives through the people."

This family sense extended even to the four male staff members. Although they could not have attended the school as students, the three male teachers (religion, math, and health) had worked at some previous time with the school principal. When job openings became available, she invited them to apply. The fourth, the school's treasurer, was married to one of the Spanish teachers.

The racial composition of the student body was overwhelmingly White, in contrast to the more diverse student racial composition of the elementary school. As at the elementary school, the St. Margaret's Academy High School family relied strongly on the myth of no internal race or class differences for its sustenance. One of the ninth-grade students, an African American girl, found this uncomfortable, although she was used to it from her experience in the elementary school. She felt alone and different. She missed the Black girls from elementary school who went elsewhere to high school, even though she loved her White friends who were still her classmates. She was surprised to see so few other Black students at the high school. Determined to do well at St. Margaret's, both socially and academically, she was confident of her future academic success but, during the first weeks of ninth grade, much less sure of her social path. For the time being, at school, her acceptance as African American by the other students depended upon her acting just as they did. There was very little variation available for a successful apprenticeship as a ninth grader, as we see in Chapter 4. She informed me that she talked differently, dressed differently, listened to different music, and so on, when she was not at school. She was not willing to become "raceless" forever. She planned to meet and become friendly with the few other Black girls in the school and to join the Black Awareness Club, although she was not sure how well accepted her membership in this club would be by her classmates. The sense of family that was talked about as an important element of community here for this student required a substantial sacrifice on her part. Although researchers have elsewhere documented similar issues regarding racial identity and success in high school, the pressure to conform to the dominant norms at St. Margaret's Academy High School included a welcome into "family" that has not been explored in those studies (Fordham, 1988; Hemmings, 1996).

The politicized borders of community membership at this school came from inside the group, in contrast to the borders imposed by the university upon the remedial writing students. One had to be willing to conform and act as if the myth of family whiteness was true. This was a perilous border, because it was recognizable only to those from whom the sacrifice was demanded. To call attention to the sacrifice, and thus make the border more visible and open to interrogation, was intolerable. Anyone calling attention to the borders ran the risk of being ostracized by fellow students and of being considered to have an "attitude." As at the elementary school, the necessity of maintaining the myth of family rendered the group vulnerable whenever the mythic aspects of their identity become visible. At the high school, however, the vulnerabilities were clearest when race became an issue.

Although the concept of family at the high school relied on the same myth that was in play at the elementary school, the nature of the sense of family at the high school was different from that at St. Margaret's Academy Elementary School or at Uptown School. Here family was evoked by the history of intergenerational attendance of the students' female relatives and a sense of tradition, of the St. Margaret's way of doing things. The important connections that meant community here were strong because they also recurred within the students' and staff's families. This contrasts to St. Margaret's Academy Elementary School and Uptown School, where a sense of family and connection was closely related to current social relationships between staff and students and among the students. The students' families mostly felt included in community at Uptown, but there had not yet been time for a sense of history to become an important aspect of community there. Parents were politely kept at a distance by the staff at St. Margaret's Elementary School and were not considered to be members of the school community.

Teacher Expectations

The way that teachers talked about their work with students revealed their beliefs about their professional identity. It also shed light on the nature of the social relations possible between teachers and students at this school. Thirteen of the high school teachers and three administrators were interviewed in October and November 1994. The teachers taught ninth-grade Latin, religion, English, guidance, social studies, biology, earth science, and mathematics. They were asked to respond to the following questions:

> What do you expect the students to be able to know and to do when they come to you in September? Do the students meet your expectations?
> What do you expect the students to know and be able to do when they leave you in June? What happens between September and June to help the students meet your expectations?
> How do you know when you, your students or the school are successful?

The teachers expected the students to exhibit a combination of general classroom behavior and specific subject competencies. The general behaviors included understanding class routines, such as being seated, taking turns, raising a hand when seeking the teacher's attention, listening silently, being friendly, courteous, and respectful to the teachers and other students. These expectations were met by almost every student. The teachers hoped, but did not always find, that the students were well-organized.

The academic behaviors expected of the students were an ability to think critically, to take notes, and to do all their work as well as possible. The teachers found variety in how well the students measured up to these expectations. They believed that which elementary school a student had attended had significant impact on the student's competence in these behaviors.

The more specific academic expectations the teachers had of the new ninth graders included basic math skills, competence in grammar and in writing, some understanding of geography, and a sense of God in their lives. Most students exhibited these competencies. Because the students came from many different elementary schools, the teachers did not presuppose that the students shared a common body of content-area knowledge.

The teachers expected the students to develop academic skills such as critical thinking, the ability to effectively communicate orally and in writing, and how to think mathematically and scientifically. The teachers expected mastery of the curriculum from all students, although their expectations for the honors students were higher.

The religion teachers spoke of spiritual rather than intellectual goals. The students were expected to be able to understand the Gospels and sacraments, to incorporate these into their lives, and to become "good Christians."

The staff listed numerous specific things that they did to ensure that these goals were met: drill and practice, frequent testing, making connections between points explicit, dictating clear and concise notes, preparing studying guides, talking about personal experience, varying modes of presentations, frequent progress reports, communication with parents, and working on organizational skills.

As did the elementary teachers, the high school teachers frequently cited student achievements as measures of their own success as well as measures of student success. Test scores were only one way of measuring success. Happy students who worked hard and were satisfied with their work were another. Seeing that students made connections and understood what was taught was important. Students who did not participate in class or who appeared unmotivated were a signal that the teacher was unsuccessful. One teacher saw improvement in student attitudes and behavior as indicative of student and teacher success. One religion teacher said, "If they leave me with some doubts and questions at the end of the year, then I've done my job. Religion has to become theirs, not mine. It can't become personal unless there is a process of questions and doubts."

In contrast to what St. Margaret's Elementary School teachers and Uptown teachers said about their schools, St. Margaret's Academy High School teachers said little about caring and connection in their interviews. These teachers talked about generic St. Margaret's High School students when they discussed their work, whereas the Uptown teachers always talked about specific students. The typical St. Margaret's Academy High School teacher was professional, brisk, competent, and focused on academics, although the religion teacher pushed her students toward a personal commitment to religious beliefs. There was apparently not much interest in the student as a whole person, despite the school's philosophy statement. Interviews with Uptown graduates indicated that teachers in their public high schools held similar attitudes, probably influenced by the organization of the schools. This detachment contrasted to the way teachers talked about their jobs and interacted with students at all of the other sites in this study. The staff at St. Margaret's Academy High School regarded themselves as professional and as being in community, but their view did not reflect the elements of staff professionalism or of community that were evidenced by staff at St. Margaret's Academy Elementary School, nor did it reflect the sense of being in professional community held by the staff of Uptown School.

Philosophy and Goals

Teaching and learning in a successful school is organized around coherent philosophy and goals. The school's formal philosophy and goals valued spiritual, intellectual, emotional, social, and physical development of human potential, private education as an alternative to public education, Gospel values, academic excellence, peace and justice, attention to the uniqueness of the individual, awareness of cultural diversity, and service.

These values were hierarchical, with spiritual development having priority over academic, social, emotional, and physical development. However, no area of development could be eliminated or ignored if the philosophy was to be carried out. The teachers were responsible for ensuring that specific goals were met through their teaching and classroom interactions with the students.

The high school's philosophy and goals resonated with those of the elementary school, particularly in the emphasis on human development, peace and justice, and Christian or Gospel values, although the high school emphatically promoted awareness and practice of the Catholic faith and values, and consequently placed less emphasis on diversity of religious beliefs. The high school was more specific in its other goals as well. Although the schools were separate entities, there was a continuity of values that reflected those of the religious congregation that sponsored both schools.

The staff was given a list of specific goals at their first staff meeting, which was the day prior to the first day of school for the students. Among the four goals listed for the 1994–95 academic year were the following:

> To strengthen our identity as members of a Catholic community who respect self, others and property by: becoming more aware and action-oriented in our efforts to eliminate racism, elitism and prejudice in our school community

The goal of eliminating racism, elitism, and prejudice in the school community was seen as an important element of being in community at the school because such attitudes conflicted with the Catholic ideology of social justice and equality based on inclusive membership in God's family. It was possible to carry out this goal without developing close and caring relationships between students and teachers, because the teachers believed that they were able to carry out the school's philosophy and goals through their classroom teaching.

SUMMARY OF THE CHAPTER

We have seen that an important task for the groups at each site was to mark themselves out as different and apart from others. The construction of group identity was talked about and accomplished differently at each site, reflecting the members' different perceptions about the nature of community at each.

Each group either constructed or recognized its identity as it went about the business of education. The deliberate creation of alternative interpretations of the remedial writing class's institutionally recognized identity was undertaken in a desperate attempt to achieve one specific goal: passing a test. Successfully enacting the idea of the group as in community depended on this transformation. The fact that internal difference and diversity was the stuff used to create the new explanations of the identity followed from the accurate perception that these had already been used to construct the stigmatizing institutional interpretations.

Uptown actively sought to create a sense of group identity and community as an important aspect of its educational mission. An idealized notion of community was frequently referenced in the words of the staff, students, and parents when describing community there. The celebration of difference and diversity was considered an important element of Uptown group identity. In support of this attitude, staff roles especially became defined to ensure a sense of professional identity and community, and certain social relations became highly valued. These social relations (trust, caring, individual attention) were elements of group identity at Uptown that contrasted to the social relations and roles perceived to exist in other public schools.

St. Margaret's Academy Elementary School considered itself to be a family securely nestled within the embrace of a spiritual family. Their essential spiritual commonality was the most important factor in both their collective identity and the social relations they enacted among themselves. As described later, minimizing the importance of certain kinds of difference and diversity made it possible to practice the tolerance of diversity that they believed marked their community as different from other groups. They believed that their tightly knit, cohesive, tolerant family was substantially different from any social organization offered by public schools.

The security and confidence of generations of community continuity produced the specific sense of family that marked St. Margaret's Academy High School. Tradition, conformity, and uniformity structured their sense of being in community. As in the Catholic elementary school, the membership within a spiritual family and, even more specifically, within a faith community with clear boundaries was the cornerstone of their collective identity. The roles of teacher and student were painstakingly defined and bordered, and in addition were structured so that current social relations did not significantly contribute to a sense of community. Tradition ruled.

At each site the creation of group identity existed in relationship to making internal difference and diversity significant or insignificant. The interstices between the construction of group and individuated identity were vulnerable spaces within community for all the groups studied. In order for the actual practices of community to come tolerably close to those of the idealized visions of community held by group participants, internal diversity and differences were made to coincide with the idealized identity that goes with idealized community. Beliefs and other practices fell within a comfort zone of variance from what was idealized.

The next chapter examines how aspects of difference and diversity are made insignificant or significant, followed by a chapter examining how members learn and celebrate the community norms that authenticate their group identity.

CHAPTER 3

The Construction
of Difference and Diversity

In all the settings, the development of the whole person was stressed. However, there were differences in understanding not only what comprises a whole person but also how the whole person and schooling can intersect. In the remedial writing class, for example, every aspect of the students' lives was considered to be importantly interconnected with their current status as students in need of remediation. Writing practice alone would not be enough to make these students successful; rather, a critical analysis of the conditions of their own lives was considered essential to their becoming real writers.

There was an important difference in the understanding of what comprises a "whole child" between Uptown and the two Catholic schools. The Catholic schools attended to four aspects of a child's development: spiritual, academic, social, and emotional. Uptown attended to three: academic, social, and emotional. As a result, consideration of the diversity of the students was a primary focus at Uptown. In both of the Catholic schools, the essential commonality of the students as members in a spiritual family was a primary focus (Blot & Calderwood, 1995).

A single set of values dominated in the Catholic schools, those of the Catholic Church. Any number of sets of values co-existed in harmony or discord at Uptown. The Catholic schools had recourse to an intact, non-negotiable moral code that could be taught to students. Uptown did not have this option available, because of the diversity of beliefs of its members. As a result, there was a wider range of acceptable student behavior at Uptown.

DIMINISHMENT OF DIFFERENCE

The diminution of the importance of perceived physical or socially constructed differences was necessary so that the tolerance of diversity claimed as an important group characteristic could be practiced at St. Margaret's Academy Elementary School.

Diversity, in order to be tolerated, had to be controlled or ignored as much as possible. For example, the economic diversity among the students' families was masked to some extent by requiring students to wear simple and inexpensive uniforms and by restricting the type and amount of jewelry the students were allowed to wear. Personal religious differences were downplayed as much as possible by the teachers and students during class time. When doctrine was taught or examined, it was that of the Catholic Church. No occasions were observed or talked about where religious differences caused tensions between students and teachers or among students. These were considered insignificant differences as far as social relations or academic curricula were concerned. Personality differences, however, were not insignificant and required the most earnest application of tolerance or remediation. At St. Margaret's, differences that were explicitly acknowledged at Uptown and in the remedial writing class (race, class, and so on) were generally publicly labeled as individual personality differences by the students and staff.

However, during conversations in the teachers' lounge at lunchtime, expressions of tolerance and appreciation for difference and diversity did not match the more public classroom performances. For example, one teacher bitterly complained about a student who extended her Christmas vacation in order to visit with relatives in South America. She disparaged the family who considered this an acceptable reason to miss a week of school. She made remarks such as "you know how they [Latino families] are." Even in the more public spaces, the practice of tolerance for difference or diversity was not always evident. For example, the first-grade teacher made several disparaging remarks to me about the family of one of her students, implying that its configuration was morally deficient. She was harsh with this student, holding the child accountable for the inappropriateness of her family. The second-grade teacher was the most vigilant in squashing outward signs of difference among her students. Every child in her class studied and practiced to receive First Communion, for example, regardless of the child's religious affiliation. Her students were the only class in the school to be entirely uniform and in uniform when school pictures were taken. All their socks were the same color, all wore navy blue cardigans, and so on. The enforcement of uniform appearance was coupled with intensive management of the movement of the children's bodies and the control of when they could and could not speak during the school day. On the surface, these students were all the same. Ethnic, linguistic, and gender differences were ignored.

One teacher acknowledged occasional tensions among her seventh-grade students that she could only conclude were racially cast. She viewed this tension as tragic and in need of remediation. Her choice was to discuss the tensions during religion class, where specific moral values (the primacy of spiritual equality, for example) could be applied to similar fictionalized problems. This transformation of what might have been significant diversity and difference into insignificance or nonexistence was necessary at St. Margaret's. Everyone had to be essentially the same in what was counted as most important and significant: being a child of God. Such transformation implies the initial recognition of these differences as significant; however, the potential social tensions associated with attending to the significance of such categories as race, gender, or social class were intolerable to the group. It may be that they were perceived to contradict, rather than support, the important and necessary emphasis on spiritual equality.

In an interview, the gym teacher at St. Margaret's illustrated how conflict is interrupted:

> When they start the bad sportsmanship and everything, you get in there quick. The language also, their attitudes toward themselves, towards other people. That you're always stressing, that's not the Catholic way, and then you bring out what should you have said, or what you should have done.

Opportunities to sort students out along race or class or gender lines were carefully monitored and controlled by staff and students. Limited opportunities to display politicized difference and diversity made the few appropriate displays safe enough to tolerate. Most of these opportunities were arranged during the month of February in conjunction with a school-wide emphasis on honoring the achievements of selected African Americans, through the display of commercial posters and a week-long series of short presentations by eighth-grade students during the school-wide morning meetings in February 1994. Similarly, the Black Awareness Club at St. Margaret's Academy High School was the only comfortably tolerable venue for attending to and displaying racial difference at St. Margaret's Academy High School. It is important to note that membership in this club was not exclusionary, and any student, whatever her ethnic or racial self-identification, was welcome to join. Thus any student's race could continue to be treated as if it were an insignificant factor, even in this club.

Attention was paid to generalized and "outside" rather than specific and internal racial or ethnic differences and diversity at St. Margaret's Academy Elementary School. These carefully arranged celebrations were the predominate channels through which diversity or difference was acknowledged. These were generally pleasant experiences for the students and teachers, several of whom told me that they found them sufficiently entertaining and educational.

This tolerance would occasionally blossom into appreciation for diversity during carefully arranged times for certain kinds of diversity and difference to be displayed. Recognition for and display of academic, artistic, or athletic achievement, talent, or skill were allowed. But the expression of self-development was not always welcomed.

An example of the latter occurred late in February 1993 when the science teacher in St. Margaret's Academy Elementary School was repeatedly challenged by a seventh-grade student during a confusing moment in the science lesson. The students and teacher were reviewing concepts to be tested the next day, and the teacher was quizzing the students about physical and chemical changes. The student insisted that painting a door caused a chemical as well as a physical change, and the teacher insisted that only a physical change was involved. The student persisted in putting forth her challenging ideas. Finally, in exasperation, the teacher told the student to memorize the dictated and uncomplicated definitions and to be prepared to use them in the upcoming test. The message sent, and at least publicly received, was that passing the test with a high grade had the greatest immediate priority. In keeping with what Henry (1968) describes elsewhere, students were expected to cooperate with the teacher by figuring out what she wanted them to do or say, and then doing and saying it. The students were expected to become "docile." This is an endeavor usually willingly undertaken by students, Henry points out, in order that they may be rewarded with the teacher's approval and love. Henry notes that it can be an exasperating and exhausting experience for students and teachers alike when they cannot or will not agree on what must be done or said. The imposition of docility upon students by some of the teachers at St. Margaret's Academy Elementary School worked in opposition to attempted displays of student discovery or creation of knowledge.

The Absence of Individualized Instruction

Whole-class lessons and activities prevailed in the classrooms of grades 1–8 in St. Margaret's Elementary School. Even during whole-class lessons when individual work was being done, every student did the same assignment. Small-group or individually paced work was occasionally assigned. But again, every group or individual often tackled the same assignment at the same time. For example, in April 1993, the sixth graders in St. Margaret's Academy all made their "Highway to Heaven" maps at the same time. Wrong turns and detours (which most assuredly did not lead to Heaven) were labeled with the names of undesirable deeds, and direct routes were labeled with the names of virtues and good deeds. A cursory inspection of the religion textbook from which the assignment was drawn revealed many of the phrases repeated on the maps. The students were all working with the same basic information, and although some had been able to develop the ideas further than others, one map was very much like another. This conformity and uniformity was exactly what the teacher wanted from the students.

Individualized lesson plans were not common at St. Margaret's. I found little evidence that teachers deviated from the curricula provided with the textbooks, either in the lesson plans, lessons, or teacher talk about their instruction practices. Any evidence of flexibility in the planned lessons was exhibited almost exclusively by the third- and fourth-grade teachers. Generally, the teachers planned and presented their lessons to the entire class at once. The teachers' expectations and requirements were explicitly detailed before the students began work. Every student in the class was assigned the same workload, took the same test, was measured by the identical standards, read the same books, and so on. With few exceptions, the students were expected to complete their class work alone and quietly. Tests were not an appropriate time for students to work together.

Despite the absence of individualized instruction or evaluation measures, attention was paid to the ways in which the information was presented and evaluated. For example, early in September 1994, the social studies teacher explained to the seventh-grade class what they would be studying during the first quarter of the school year, what materials would be used, and what work they would be expected to produce as evidence of their learning. They would also be expected to complete extensive written homework, take an exam after every other textbook chapter, make an oral report, and take an end-of-unit written exam.

The teacher explained to me that by varying the class activities and evaluation materials, she could give every student an opportunity to shine in at least one area. Different learning preferences would be taken into account, and students weak in any area would not be judged solely in that area. Although no student was excused from participation in every exercise, and all students were graded on the same basis, the teacher believed that the curriculum was as accessible to all students as she was able to arrange. She told me that it was her responsibility to teach to every child, although it was not possible for her to do this for every child at every moment in the school day, week, or year. Thus she arranged many opportunities for her students to be graded on performance and demonstration of knowledge. This precluded any one assessment from unduly influencing the student's grade.

This way of managing different student capabilities ensured an acceptably organized classroom and a manageable workload for the teacher. This approach to classroom management and workload can make teaching simpler for the teacher than one that stresses individualized lessons, assignments, expectations, and evaluations for each student.

The school provided an essentialized common curriculum that extended access to what Delpit (1993) calls the "culture of power" to all its students (see also Bryk et al., 1993). The teachers and administrators were explicit about what had to be done or learned, how to learn and use information and skills, and why these were important. They believed that school was the site of a necessary apprenticeship period that would prepare the student to make her or his way in the world. Frequent reference to this understanding of education was made when cautioning the students about what to expect in high school. Teachers supported these minutely detailed demands with confidence. For example, when the eighth graders began the first day of their second trimester of religion class for the year, they were told: "Open your notebooks to the next clean page and fold the page in half." So began the review of rules for good notebook management. The teacher supported her directions with the information that high school teachers expected the students to come to high school with competent note-taking skills and appropriate notebook organization. High school teachers don't teach students how to do this, she warned, and are not lenient if the student does not keep a well-organized notebook. So the students were instructed to be neat, to label everything, to number pages, date their notes, and get notes from a friend when absent. In addition to being good preparation for high school, these practices would make it easier to study for tests and consequently earn high grades. The first day of the second trimester was a logical time to review these instructions, which were the same ones the teacher had given the students the first week of school.

Simply being explicit, however, about what is expected and why it is important is not necessarily sufficient to make students believe what the teachers say and then act accordingly. At St. Margaret's, the teachers told me that they sincerely believed that they acted for the benefit of the students, that they taught what was important, and that they did so with nurturing and caring attitudes. The students said that they felt this caring and nurturing, that they respected their teachers and received respect from these teachers. The teachers told me that they respected each other's professionalism and stated that they learned from each other. The principal took pride in the close and familial relationships, believed that the individual needs of the students were met, and had confidence that the students experienced their learning as fun. Parents believed the school was academically excellent, promoted desirable morals and values, and had discipline; they likewise trusted that their children received individual attention from a caring and competent staff. This combination of beliefs supported the "trusting relations" that make learning possible within a classroom (Erickson, 1987; McDermott, 1977). Everybody believed, in concert, that the entwined enterprise of learning and teaching as it was configured at St. Margaret's was in the best interests of the students. This faith supports teacher and student engagement in their work, a sign of effective schools (Bryk et al., 1993; Lee, Bryk, & Smith, 1993).

MAKING DIVERSITY IMPORTANT

The director of Uptown School, in her address to the students during the all-school meeting on the first day of school in September 1994, described the school as a community and supported her remarks about behavior, goals, and so on, with references to the group as a community. During her initial address to the students at Uptown School, she stressed that each person was there because he or she had chosen to become a member of this school/community.

In Uptown School, the members were continually engaged in balancing the development and well-being of individuals with the development and well-being of the whole community. One teacher wrote, "I believe the balance between protecting the interests of individual students and the interests of the whole school community are delicately intertwined. In most cases you cannot do one without doing the other." So attending to the needs of the individual students is a practice that creates and sustains a community that holds such attention as a central cohering value. Embedded within each instance of working to meet an individual's needs was the articulation of community as it was understood at Uptown. As one staff member wrote, one true measure of the successful articulation of community at Uptown lies with the graduates:

> The returning students like to come back to visit. This shows that we treat them well. Many kids return to visit us. Maybe the family environment here is special. This is missing in high school, even in the small places. They keep missing us. This is more than a good place to be. The students see something here that they didn't find in elementary school, and don't find in high school. I'm not sure what it is . . . it's like missing your family. They don't realize it until they leave. It's like the way you realize you miss your own family, your home, only after you leave.

The above words highlight a deep commitment to making their curriculum "student driven and vital." This responsibility to the students was carried out in a number of ways. Teacher roles were organized to support a collective group identity as a caring community devoted to the well-being of every member through the attention they lavished upon individual students. As at St. Margaret's Academy Elementary School, much of this work was accomplished in the classrooms, where formal learning and teaching took place. However, there were significant differences between the two schools in the organization of teaching and learning with regard to difference and diversity. Where commonality, conformity, and uniformity were stressed at St. Margaret's, individuality, expressiveness, and exploration were encouraged at Uptown.

Each staff member was an advisor to about 12 students and met almost every student in one of his or her classes during the course of the academic year. Every staff member knew virtually every student, and some, notably the director and the secretary, knew students and their families quite well. Each teacher designed his or her own curriculum in humanities, science, or both, as well as in a variety of elective courses. All staff members, including the secretary, coach, and administrative assistant, taught at least one class in addition to their advisory classes. As part of the formal curriculum of the school, advisors and their groups of students formally met together for 45 minutes three times weekly. The content of the conversations and work conducted during advisory periods ranged from official school business such as report-card talk, course selection, and appropriate behavior to more personal matters such as talking about feelings, family life, and personal problems.

At Uptown School, the teachers organized their teaching so that instruction was individualized to the greatest extent they could manage. Although this was accomplished differently by different teachers, there was a consistency evident in their consideration for the unique needs of each student. Because the range of acceptable student behaviors was greater at Uptown than at St. Margaret's, teaching and learning looked different here—noisier, less coherent, more exciting. To illustrate, the following brief vignettes taken from my field notes provide a glimpse of a typical workday for two Uptown teachers.

Mr. Campbell is a white man in his middle forties who had been teaching for more than twenty years. He has been at Uptown since its beginning, and helped develop its curriculum and mission. His classroom is one of a suite of two large rooms reached through a narrow, winding corridor that begins at the far corner of the gym. The room holds about thirty student desks, all facing the front of the room. At the front of the room is a large desk that faces the student desks. There is an overhead projector on the desk, a blackboard on the wall behind it, and a large, locked closet to the left of the desk. Mr. Campbell uses this desk when teaching math. In the rear of the classroom, in one corner, is another large desk. He eats his lunch and does his paperwork here. Nearby is a large locked closet, and a tall bookcase stuffed with books. There is a Macintosh computer in the other corner of the rear of the classroom. Students' projects are displayed on the walls.

8:45 A.M. Class has officially begun. Students are quiet, although scattered subdued conversation can be heard. The teacher, at the blackboard in the front of the classroom, calls on students to dictate the steps needed to solve the problem. No student volunteers for this. The teacher calls out names. Students raise their hands to ask questions, or to comment on the process, particularly if they do not agree with the steps being dictated. The teacher calls Louise to the blackboard to work out the next problem. She quickly works it out, then turns and talks it through to the class. They had done the problem as well, in their notebooks. The students generally appear attentive, alternately watching Louise and glancing at their notebooks. Mr. Campbell compliments her work, and she returns to her seat. As she does, some students also compliment her work. A problem from the homework becomes the focus. One student is selected to give the answer. The teacher verifies that it is the correct answer. Then George raises his hand and suggests another answer. The teacher says maybe he is right. They both check, and find that George has discovered yet another correct answer to the problem. The teacher thanks George for his contribution.

The atmosphere during the class period was one of industry. The teacher and many students seemed to enjoy the session. It appeared that many of the students found the work intellectually stimulating, although not every student seemed so enthusiastic. Asking questions about the work was supported by Mr. Campbell and not once was treated as an interruption. In fact, if a student disagreed with a solution, or had arrived at it differently, she or he was expected to make that public. If a student did not understand something, she or he was expected to bring that up publicly as well. The teacher regularly asked students if they had questions or comments if no one volunteered any first. When Louise worked out her problem, the students verbally praised her, as did the teacher. They also questioned her, as if she were the teacher, if they did not understand or agree with a step she took. When George proposed his alternate solution, Mr. Campbell received his comments with an open admission that he did not know if George's answer could be right or wrong. He publicly sought additional information and worked the problem through, step by step, using the new perspective. He thanked George for sharing his insight. Not incidentally, he acknowledged that he himself had learned something new and transmitted to his students the intellectual satisfaction that can bring. This example stands in sharp contrast to the uncomfortable conversation about chemical changes between the seventh grader and her teacher at St. Margaret's Academy Elementary School described earlier. My field notes continue:

10:25. The classroom is full of students, most of whom are seated. Mr. Campbell is placing items on the front desk. There is loud talking among the students. The teacher tells the students to prepare their data sheets. He lists the equipment they will need for the activity: One nickel, one plastic cup, a balloon, some toothpicks. The teacher states that the object of the experiments that the students will do is to prove the existence of static electricity. The students have been instructed to work in pairs. The first task is to stand the nickel on its side. All students stay seated, except for the two who are distributing toothpicks. There are bursts of loud conversation as the students balance their nickels, and there are many slapping sounds as the nickels fall over. The teacher stands at his desk briefly, then walks around, observing and advising. Mr. Campbell tells the students to write a learning statement now about balancing the nickels. He talks about static electricity as he demonstrates how a charged balloon held over the plastic cup moves the toothpicks balanced on the nickels within. He calls on some students to explain the steps of the experiment. Then, the teacher gives out the balloons to the students so they can do the entire experiment. The noise level increases significantly as the kids start playing with the balloons. The balloons are blown up, loudly, air escapes, loudly, balloons fly, loudly. Everybody appears to be having fun. Mr. Campbell is laughing as he walks around the room, watching the students. Elliot and Allie successfully complete their experiment several times. The teacher says to the students, "If you have completed your experiment, write your observations and conclusions." Some students write, some continue their experiments, others are apparently playing. Meanwhile, Mr. Campbell is taking projects out of the front closet, student-designed pontoon boats with motors, variously made of wood or Styrofoam. Gloria presents her boat to the class, which is quite different from the ones seen so far. Hers is a very large military boat. The teacher lavishes compliments about the originality of the project. Finally, it is Charles's turn. His work is the only unfinished project shown. The teacher comments on the many hours of work Charles has put into the project. There is some concern voiced by students about the boat's ability to float, since it is so heavy. They suggest adding Styrofoam pontoons to the bottom to make it more buoyant.

The mood of this class was playful and relaxed. Yet the students were actively engaged in their scientific inquiry. Although this was a highly structured activity, students had multiple opportunities to converse about topics other than the lesson and more than a usual amount of space in which to move around. Some student behaviors were acceptable to the teacher in this class that were not tolerated in the math classes. Loud conversation and increased student mobility are two examples, calling out to the teacher is another, and a wider range of conversational topics is yet another. In spite of the increased opportunities for students to move and talk, there were limits for such behaviors. Although students may have known when these limits were breached, the teacher was the one who made the limits of behavior the momentary focus of attention.

Other teachers at Uptown focused on individual students in a manner different from Mr. Campbell's. For example, Ms. Wilson arranged to spend most of her time working as a facilitator for individualized student projects. My field notes illustrate:

Ms. Wilson was an energetic white woman in her mid-forties who has been teaching for four years. Her classroom is one of a suite of two rooms reached through a narrow winding corridor that begins at the intersection just past the office. The room holds about thirty student desks and chairs and two large teacher desks. The student desks are clustered in groups of four. There are two computers in the room, and several large bookcases stuffed with books. Almost every available space is covered with posters, collages, and mobiles, evidence of student work. The effect is powerful; this room is a place for student-centered work:

8:35 A.M. Humanities class has begun. Ms. Wilson is lecturing to the students about her expectations for the rough drafts of the students' projects, which are due today. Lunch at "The Cafe" is indicated for any student whose work is not ready. They will work on their projects under her supervision during the lunch hour. Ms. Wilson inquires of each student individually about the progress of their reports, and invites many to lunch at The Cafe. Students are told to take out their research, notes, books, everything they have for their project work. Ms. Wilson decides that the class will move to the office since so many students need to use the computers. Some students are instructed to remain in the classroom, in order to use the resources there. Ms. Wilson tells the students who remain behind to work and to come into the office if they need her. They are "On their honor for best behavior."

Ms. Wilson hustles to the office where there are ten students already seated at the computers. Three students are seated at the rear table, waiting to conference with her. Ms. Wilson quietly conferences with the students at the small table one at a time. She holds one girl's written work, reads it, makes comments and then listens as the student shows her another paper and speaks about it. While the girl leafs through her book, the teacher reads the proffered paper, then they resume conversation. After a few minutes, Ms. Wilson gets up and walks over to the computer bank to check on the progress of the other students. Near the computer stations, the teacher pulls up 2 chairs and calls Ellen over to her. While Ms. Wilson is editing and reading Ellen's printout, Ellen goes to assist another student at the computer. At 9:15, the teacher begins to conference with Ellen, "This is really wonderful, you've done a lot of work." Ms. Wilson explains her editorial markings to Ellen. Ellen states, "I'm not a very good writer." Ms. Wilson encourages her. Ms. Wilson gently challenges Ellen to explain a statement— pushing her to further develop her work.

As can be seen from the moments described above, there were many opportunities arranged during the day for students to work independently on their own projects or together on shared work. There were opportunities for recognition of achievement to be rendered and for individualized instruction to be given by the teacher. This atmosphere contrasts with that found at St. Margaret's Academy Elementary and High Schools.

FINDING COMMON GROUND IN DIFFERENCE

Written, signed, and oral conversations during the remedial writing class at Urban U. presented many opportunities for the students and teachers to consider their own differences and diversity. Establishing a sense of community supported by a sense of commonality was accomplished through these explorations. Unlike at St. Margaret's, where essential commonality overwhelmed superficial difference, in the writing class a commonality was created from important differences. Unlike at Uptown, difference and diversity were not enrichments to the students' development so much as they were stigmata to be transformed into honor. This transformation, however, was often incidentally accomplished during events that had other manifest functions, such as pursuing an emergent friendship. For example, during a written conversation with John, a hearing Jamaican native in his mid-30s who has spoken Jamaican Creole all his life, Denise passionately discussed her personal reactions to the autobiography they both had read of Malcolm X. Their discussion centered on racism:

Denise: I want to asking you a question about your skin color. Have dark
  skin treated you shit of your light skin or say bad thing about your
  skin. have you feel conflicts of your skin and dark skin people and
  white people.
    You know our black people have accept white people in our social
  people no matter how white people treat us hell because we have been
  experience with racial.
John: NO I HAVE NEVER EXPERIENCED IT BUT I HAVE PEOPLE
  SAID THAT I THINK I AM BETTER THAN THEM BECAUSE
  OF HOW I LOOKED.
Denise: How do you feel when they think that you look better
John: I THINK THAT ALL PEOPLE ARE BRAIN WASHED AT SOME
  IN LIFE. THE THING TO DO IS TO KNOW THE TRUTH
  ABOUT OUR BLACK HISTORY AND BE AWARE OF WHAT IS
  TRUE OR FALSE.
Margaret: John, who does the brainwashing?
Denise: I have been experience with white people and Black people about
  my skin. White people of my friend considered me as white people so
  they can talked with me about bad things black people. They know
  that I come from black person but they dont care it. and black people
  jealous of my skin because I look good too and they think I always like
  be with white people.
John: I HAD NO PROBLEMS WITH ANYONE BECAUSE I WAS AN
  ONLY CHILD, AND I NEEDED TO HAVE A FEW FRIENDS. I

HAD TO LEARN TO MAKE PEOPLE BE FRIENDLY TOWARDS
ME AS MUCH AS POSSIBLE.

As is evident from Margaret's question, this ENFI conversation was not
private. Every member of the class could monitor the conversation and observe how Denise and John discussed their common experiences with racism.
This conversation between Denise, deaf, and John, hearing, was one of many
such conversations (written, signed, and oral) in which the students explored
common experiences and learned that they were alike in many important ways.
Such conversations carried out some of the work that Sharon and Margaret
urged the students to undertake: to discover and examine a common theme
of struggle in their lives.

VOICE AND SILENCING

Dissent and consensus are intertwined within community. Harmony within
community is dependent upon balancing dissent and consensus so that dissent does not rip community apart, nor does consensus rip apart enriching
differences. This balancing task imposes limitations on the manifestation of
the voice of the individual members. Voice (Bakhtin, 1981; Volosinov, 1973;
Wertsch, 1991) is the speaking personality of the individual. But it is misleading to consider that an individual has a single, unadulterated voice; it is blended
with at least one other at all times. One's own voice (not just the speaking
voice but also thought and inner speech) is always engaged in a dialogue with
another, anticipating and responding to the other even in solitary reverie. Voice
itself is solidly grounded in interpersonal activity, and the very structure of inner
speech reflects this dynamic interchange. An internalized heterogeneity of
voices results from the demand on individuals to learn and use a multiplicity
of appropriate voices/languages (genres, registers, languages, idioms, clichés,
etc.) in daily life. Sansom (1982) writes of the practice of an aboriginal group
with regard to the ownership of the right to speak of illness, an event that is
assumed to leave an indelible, crippling stigma of some sort (for example, a
stutter, a limp) on its survivor. But the afflicted individual is never granted the
voice to speak of her or his own illness. The management of the illness, the
worrying, the concern, the caretaking, and the mourning, belongs to the entire community, and one of the community members is granted the voice and
the responsibility to speak of the illness. This is a responsibility to the entire
community, not to particular individuals. Sharon, the teacher of the remedial
writing class, often spoke for her students in a similar manner. But Sharon's
habit of elaborating on the comments of others may have undermined her
efforts to give voice to the community members:

But this is one of our battles, right? Many of us in this room belong to groups of people who have silenced voices, right? Not silent, but silenced, you know—"-E-D" [sic], meaning that it has been for many economic or social or educational reasons. You have to find your own voice. And that's what you have to do, right?

Silencing voice can be accomplished through appropriation and transformation of a marginalized voice (Fine, 1987; Sola & Bennett, 1985). It seems that Sharon, through her appropriation and transformation of the voices of the students, may have denied them the raising of their own voices and, consequently, their sense of personal efficacy. Gino, hard of hearing, was by far the least articulate member of the community and seldom spoke during the class discussions. Sharon, however, regularly attempted to draw him into the discussions, and would supply his part when he failed to do so himself. For example:

Sharon: Gino, you want to say something.
Gino: Huh?
Sharon: How was the reading for you?
Gino: It was all right.
Sharon: Did you learn something new from reading? You read Helen Keller's *My Life*, right?
Gino: Mmm.
Sharon: Did you learn something new that you could relate to?
Gino: Uh Uh [Meaning no].
Sharon: You do. You do. But you find it hard to say it.
Gino: Yeah.
Sharon: Remember you said, in one of your papers. You're from an Italian family. Remember what I said to you? What does that mean? What does your family do for you? What do they do in that culture to help you get through?
Gino: I don't remember.
Sharon: I do! That was key. He said all this in the paper, right? He said that we're a very close family, and maybe we're close because we're Italian. And that has a lot to do with our cultures, right? That your family is very close. Because people look out, look after each other. And you said that your sisters and brothers all live nearby. You see each other all the time. You talk about your brother all the time, right—Ned?
Gino: Yeah.
Sharon: Who's been the person who got you through everything, right? Everything. He got you tutors, he never let you give up.

Gino: He said, " go on, go on."
Sharon: And that's very important that a lot of us come from cultures like
that. Sometimes we forget, right?

Speaking for Gino accomplished several ends. Sharon would leave no
participant out of that particular conversation; it was important for everyone
there to contribute in a personally revealing way. When Gino could not, or
would not, do this himself, she did it for him. Because one of the purposes of
the conversation was to ascertain if the students had internalized and believed
the message that they were indeed a community of real writers, it was important for all to say that they had done so. And, as is shown by the turn the ex-
changes took, Gino was coerced into participating as he did.

One of the interesting things about this exchange was that Sharon knew
that Gino did not write the paper to which she referred. His brother Ned functioned as Gino's ghost writer outside class, and Sharon voiced for him in class.
He was never expected by the teachers to be able to pass the WAT; he had
been misplaced into the class because of his status as hard of hearing. Still, he
was allowed to remain because he was not disruptive to the establishment of
the community of writers. He was a passive, nonwriting, nonvoicing member
of the community. He had a continuing role in the community because his
outstanding inarticulateness cast the other students as comparatively articulate and competent. Later in the semester, Gino told me that he hated the
college and was there only to please his brother. He found it oppressively difficult. He called the experience boring, and it was obvious that he tuned out
most of the class discussions, yet he seldom missed a class.

Sharon's apparent ventriliquizing for Gino is also an instance of using a
spoken text to demonstrate, and thus normalize, a particularly desired attitude toward accomplishment, that is, one that acknowledges interdependence,
trust, helpfulness, and dependency. Gino, in the spotlight, found no space to
argue against this attitude, as his only option was to assent to Sharon's words.
It was not important that he actually agree or add in any substantial way to
the conversation. What was important was that there was no space, no possibility to do other than assent to her use of his written text in this manner
(McDermott, 1988).

As a late semester discussion between Sharon, Margaret, and me ended,
I asked Sharon if she was aware of the magnitude of her presence in the classroom. Citing Freire (1985) and Shor (1989), she spoke to me of the necessarily strong role of the teacher. However, Freire (1985) cautions, "There is a
radical difference, though, between being present and being the presence itself"
(p. 105). Sharon, as a critical analyst of pedagogy (both her own and others),
recognized the contradictions implied in "empowering" her students (Lather,
1991). Her agency simultaneously enabled and disabled her students in their

movement toward the sometimes contradictory goals of self-recognition and academic progress.

In the act of giving voice, a great silence continued to be sustained. Within this silenced space, there was room to understand another of their common experiences—that one did not necessarily have to be biologically deaf or mute in order to be rendered incommunicado. The tragic commonality of their isolation from and invisibility to the mainstream of the university still existed, no matter how they came to think of themselves. The border imposed from outside was vast.

The "Zone of Silence"

In addition to the imposition of silence upon a group from outside, there are also opportunities within community to impose a silence upon group members in the service of preserving and honoring community values and norms. At St. Margaret's Academy Elementary School, for example, exhibitions of disruptive or unresolvable difference seldom occurred. Students and staff learned how to be good and appropriate, which precluded most potential problems. Among the mechanisms of ensuring appropriate talk was the retreat into the "zone of silence."

This zone of silence ensured an absence of potential divisive talk about what were considered to be sensitive subjects, some of which were deemed to be proprietary to the students' families, and some of which were considered to be moral issues about which the Catholic Church holds sacrosanct beliefs. Because this is a private Catholic school, not a diocesan school, it could, to some degree, avoid embarrassing the non-Catholic students or making them feel cast out of community by eliminating potentially controversial discussions.

One teacher and some of the 1993 eighth graders described such a zone. Some subjects—sexuality, for example—were not considered appropriate and were never discussed, according to the students. Naturally, said the students, these were the very subjects they longed to explore. The teacher understood such a prohibition as one that allowed her to keep her job, as she was never troubled by any clashes between her personal beliefs and those that were orthodox. She simply could not discuss them with the students at all.

One afternoon, the eighth-grade social studies class examined the Bill of Rights. The content of their discussion concerned current examples of utilization of the Bill of Rights. One student wanted to include the topic of abortion for consideration. In response, the teacher said, "You [kids] can address this, but we can't do it here." As an alternative, the teacher, using questions, prodded the students to decide which of the rights and amendments were utilized in the process of accusing, capturing, and trying an accused criminal. The students persisted in asking tough questions. One girl wanted to know what rights were involved in the personal use of illegal drugs. The brief examination of this topic was supported by the teacher. The discussion continued as the topic switched to separation of church and state, with specific regard to taxes. The principal, whose office adjoined the classroom, was invited inside to speak about the school's tax responsibilities. She gave information and agreed with the students and teacher that the topic was interesting.

Although the principal was nearby and had very likely heard the entire discussion, including the questions about abortion and illegal drug use, she did not comment on anything until she was invited to do so. She did not interrupt the class. The teacher was the person who reminded the students of their zone of silence. However, as this teacher had remarked to me in September, the proximity of the principal to her classroom had an inhibiting effect on her class discussions. In other words, the discussion about abortion may or may not have been curtailed quite so sharply if the teacher and students had had more privacy. Perhaps there might have been some listing of the competing rights that mark the abortion issue. It should also be noted that in 1993–94, this teacher designed and implemented a course for the eighth graders that dealt with some of the otherwise "zoned out" issues—most notably, drug and alcohol abuse awareness and prevention. Everything done and said when this course was conducted was confidential.

The group at Uptown School, having no recourse to a zone of silence such as that in play at St. Margaret's Academy Elementary School, found no topic taboo for discussion in class or in staff meetings. Because even the most uncomfortable subjects were acceptable for explicit consideration, strategies for dealing with discomfort were developed. One frequently traveled avenue was the management of consensus and its corollary, dissent.

Consensus

Direct and clear rules about appropriate talk and beliefs were the norm at St. Margaret's Academy Elementary School. At Uptown School, in contrast, any topic was ostensibly appropriate for talk, and any sincerely held belief was, in theory, respected. But it was important for the staff to find a way to reconcile their different beliefs in order to go on with their business of making decisions and attending to the needs of individual students. The idea and practice of consensus became important.

Shared assumptions, either examined or not, made daily practices possible at Uptown. For example, the staff assumed a "shared fiction" that the decisions they made together were consensual. The operational understanding of consensus at the school was that every person had an opportunity to have a voice in the process, and that there was agreement that decisions were reached and supported by all. Vanderberghe and Staessens (1991) call this consensus "vision." This is not to say that there was agreement among the staff as to the exact nature of the shared beliefs and values, and most especially not to say that staff practices paralleled each other. In particular, the belief that all were committed to "the kids" fostered further assumptions, some supported and some not, about other shared values, beliefs, and practices. Even when significant disagreement among them about these was obvious, the basic assumption that "they are all there for the kids" encouraged the staff to act as if in concert. Vanderslice (1995) writes that sharing such beliefs leads group members to believe that they also share attitudes. Rosenholtz (1989) writes that a school's effectiveness substantially depends on the consensus of the staff's beliefs about their work, their shared goals, management of students, and so on. Greater concert among these beliefs is, according to Rosenholtz, closely correlated with more effective schooling. However, as we will see, on close examination such concert may reveal substantial variability in beliefs, values, and practices.

Some teachers described their assumptions about shared beliefs this way:

Teaching kids is one of the most important jobs in the world. That the school be as diverse as possible ethnically, racially, religiously, economically, and in ability. That we provide "equity" as far as possible (i.e., material provided at school for kids who do not have them at home). That consensual decision-making is important to teach and live by. That all adults and kids are both learners and teachers.

We all believe that we're changing things, although there are different notions of what that is. We believe the public system has failed people. We all feel that we have input to a certain degree, although there are different levels. We believe we do good. We believe we provide value. We each think the others do good things for the school, are committed to kids, and work hard. We believe all this even though we know we have major differences.

Groups that share important core beliefs tend to generalize this concord; they ascribe more far-reaching accord about all matters than may actually exist. For example, there were assumptions among the Uptown staff that they shared understandings about consensus, democracy, leadership, authority, and accountability. However, subtle and sometimes sharp ideological differences existed among and between groups of parents, staff, and students. For example, different teachers cited Dewey, Freire, and Coalition of Essential Schools principles as indicative of their educational philosophies, yet these philosophies are not necessarily compatible (Dewey, 1990/1900; Freire, 1985; Sizer, 1992). As an example, consider the proscription, embodied in the "essential questions," that is inherent in the coalition's principles. Contrast this with the Freirean process of "conscientization," which situates the development of curriculum within a critical examination of one's position in a social hierarchy. The first presupposes an agreement (recognized or not) to continue in the tradition of a particular type of academic knowledge. The second demands a transformation of what counts as knowledge. A Deweyian framework presupposes a construction by the child of a set of knowledge that builds on, rather than transforms, existing modes of knowledge. A child's classroom is the "world," in the Deweyian understanding, and the child, as actor, actively constructs the social world as she or he learns. The coalition model narrowly restricts what is studied, in contrast to the Deweyian model. It does not account for the critical consciousness that challenges and changes the world in the Freirean model. Each model was developed for a different population as well, in age or social status, for example. This is not to say that different teachers within one school cannot find ways to accommodate each other's preference for the fundamental principles of one model or another but only that accomplishing such compatibility may not always be possible, and may not always be attempted.

Uptown staff members have described consensus at the school in these ways:

> We talk. We think about what we talked about. We talk some more. We stumble around trying to understand each other. It has happened that we have been unable to come to consensus. We are uncomfortable when that happens. When we do arrive at consensus there is a sense of celebration in the room.

> I think consensus is really "compromise." There are too many dissenting opinions to agree, but eventually (after long discussion) a decision is arrived at.

In reviewing decisions made during staff meetings, it became evident that the beliefs about consensus were not always supported by the data. Sometimes staff members were absent when decisions were made. Staff members sometimes kept silent about their disagreement with the prevailing ideas. Staff members with minority viewpoints regularly stated disagreement with decisions only after the fact, disavowing, disclaiming affiliation, critiquing, impeding, or demanding changes in the decisions. The first year of the research project, in fact, teachers of color were frequently critical of the prevailing practices but often did not speak up at the decision table. They intended their silence to communicate dissent, but this was not acknowledged. The potential power of their silence (Basso, 1972; Tannen, 1994) was diminished because it

did not evoke a significant response in their audience. Their critiques consequently were not addressed by the staff together. According to the director, efforts
were made to encourage the silent to talk but were seldom accepted. These silent dissenters reserved much of their critique for my ears, and for each other.

Because the staff's operating definition of consensus included not only
the opportunity to voice but also the reaching of agreement, agreement was
often inferred or assumed in the decision-making processes outlined earlier.
The silence was not understood to break consensus; rather, silence was consent and agreement. This excerpt, from the director's memo to the staff, provides an example of how agreement to the decisions and to the director's right
to make these decisions was assumed:

> Please set aside at least an hour or two to read, think about, and react
> to the enclosed. Call me with comments, questions, and any disagree-
> ments. Since we didn't have the usual summer retreat, I have put
> together a lot of important information and made some decisions with
> the input of those around. If I don't hear from you, I will assume you
> are comfortable with everything.

Although, in theory, every member of the staff had the right and responsibility to voice his or her opinions and to participate with equal power in the
decision-making processes, this is not what happened. The director, for example, bore an unequal responsibility and accountability to the school dis-
trict, and along with these, much of the power and influence over decisions.
To take another example, the school secretary, respected and beloved by the
school community, did not participate with equal authority with the teachers
in decision-making conversations, although she was an advisor for 12 students,
taught the Spanish class, and was the primary liaison between the school and
the neighborhood parents, many of whom were not fluent in English. She was
often silent during meetings, although at one meeting she took the floor to
describe the discussions she and her advisory group had had about the meanings of discipline. However, my field notes show that when she finished speaking out that day, the facilitator immediately moved on to the next agenda item.
The staff did not spend time discussing her findings, although some teachers
did follow her lead in their own advisories later. Not only did the staff share
unequally in decision-making processes, but also nonstaff parents and students
did not attend staff meetings at all. This is consistent with current literature
that notes the absenting of parental participation in traditional and alternative schools (Giles, 1995; Graves, 1995; Moore, 1992).

As noted earlier, having voice, an essential constituent of consensus for
the staff, was translated to mean that all had the opportunity to speak and to
be heard. Having the opportunity to speak was tantamount to having voice,

whether or not one participated in the conversation orally or silently. During decision-making conversations, only spoken words carried the reciprocal obligation of listening. Consequently, the eloquence of silence was often lost somewhere along the many paths through which one might or might not have participated in decision-making. As Vanderslice (1995) notes in her study of other cooperative groups, speaking up is considered to be a key responsibility of the participants, for it makes available to the group the rich benefits of its own diversity. Although public disagreement might result, the group's responsibility in turn is to work through any such disagreement. Holding a silence can be understood as well then as an abdication of one's responsibility to the group, for it precludes the group's opportunity to collectively and cooperatively work through the dissent or difference.

At Uptown, when staff members believed that their voices would not be heard, they sometimes acted as if in consensus with the dominant group but then engaged in activities that undermined the consensus (Calderwood, in press-a). As Johnson and Johnson (1987) have noted, this type of discordant participation is a common occurrence when group members perceive that they have been forced into acceptance of ostensible group decisions with which they do not concur and, more important, from which their full participation has been precluded.

Dissent

Despite the strong normative force compelling consensus or the illusion of consensus, dissension was an important aspect of the reflective practice that the Uptown staff considered vital to the community's continued existence (Calderwood, in press-a). Each time difference was explicitly laid out and examined through dissension or discussion, the opportunities for strengthening or fracturing the community were available to be chosen. The same opportunities were available when explicit examination of differences was avoided, although the avoidance of direct and open discussion posed more risk for fracture than for resilience. At times, both options resulted, with fractures of resentment and feeling silenced balanced or outweighed by the belief that new understandings had been forged, and all had been heard. I have elsewhere extensively examined the role of dissension in creating professional identity during what I have come to call "the decision dance" at Uptown (Calderwood, in press-a). Here, however, I look at the vulnerabilities made visible by one way that dissension during decision-making was addressed at Uptown.

Dissension was often managed with interruptions that occurred when conversations became too uncomfortable to sustain, particularly when competing values and beliefs were laid bare or when cherished beliefs about what was in practice in the school were shown to be mistaken. The form of the interruption varied from a reminder that the staff had many other items to which they must attend, a criticism of the words or interpretations being offered, or the presentation of an alternative and more generally acceptable interpretation.

One interruption began when a staff person disagreed with a stated point of view that appeared to criticize the school or to potentially wound it. The disagreement was clearly stated, then followed by a passionate description, a reminder, of the school's philosophy and ideology, illustrated by examples of how these were well supported by specific practices. This was an ordinary and frequent occurrence, which was not given much thought by the staff. When such an interruption did occur, remarks often attributed it to a personality quirk of the interrupter. Because the attributing of personal characteristics as influential factors is a common way that people understand the behaviors of others, but not themselves (Jones & Nisbett, 1972; Kihlstrom, Marchese-Foster, & Klein, 1997), it interfered with the accurate analysis of the power relations that factored into the working through of differences during decision discussions at Uptown.

The particular type of interruption held up, and held safe, a picture of shared values and beliefs that folded together to characterize the school. It described the idealized school as if lived. It was meant as a healing and protective gesture as well as an interruption.

Unfortunately, however, it also cut off dissension that may be a necessary component of democratic decision-making. Dissension voiced by staff was more often viewed as potentially or actually an instance of fracturing of the school community than as an important aspect of democratic practice (Calderwood, 1997). As Mansbridge (1996) writes, the use of coercive power is sometimes a necessary element of democracy, in order that daily business actually gets done. As long as this coercion is actively and consistently critiqued and challenged, it is still possible to maintain democracy in decision-making. However, this democratically necessary dissension voiced by Uptown staff was more often viewed as potentially or actually an instance of fracturing of the school community than as an important aspect of democratic practice (Calderwood, 1997). Thus it was consistently interrupted.

At Uptown, a reluctance to recognize aspects of the school culture that sustained or allowed problems to occur was an area of vulnerability (Calderwood, in press-a). Their focus on individual students usually omitted an examination of how the student's behavior made sense within the school culture, or how it was part of a larger pattern of behaviors that were supported by the school culture (Blot, personal communication, 1995; McDermott, 1994). This is a classic example of the fundamental attribution error (Brehm & Kassin, 1990; Jones & Nisbett, 1972; Schon, 1995) by which people understand the behaviors of others as primarily due to personal, rather than situational, factors. Many discussions and decisions were confidential, and particularly sensitive ones often did not include the whole staff. Without cumulative record-keeping of similar events, it was difficult to see possible systemic patterns that transcended individual student behavior. Frequency and pervasiveness were difficult to track. The absence of such comprehensive record-keeping served at least one aspect of the school's mission. It forced a "unique," "singular," "individual student" interpretation of what, in the absence of irrefutable evidence, could not be seen as a moment within a set of similar moments, as a moment within a systemic pattern. A similar process was used at St. Margaret's Academy Elementary School.

When the staff spoke of school-wide issues, such as the general behavior of students, the role of the school culture in shaping the issues was considered secondary to that of individual actors at specific moments. But the examination of the school culture itself seldom occurred in the course of discussing an individual student. Rather, it was generally considered only when the conversation began with the presentation of an issue, such as discipline, and not when it began with the discussion of particular problems of a specific student. Even then, moves were made to limit the examination of the role of the school culture. If larger social forces were considered, they were considered as originating outside the school culture and imported into the school. For example, during a 20-minute discussion of generalized problems with student behaviors, one teacher commented:

> There's just a whole lot of, people have problems, you know. Life, life is hard. I mean, there's a recession this year for most of us. And it's still here for most of us. And I think it's probably true of parents and families that we're talking about. And I think there's a lot of pain in the world right now. Who can bear to watch another news story about Sarajevo? It looks hopeless! And I think one of the things we're kind of absorbing, I guess, is that the kids that we're trying to help prepare for their own kind of future, and it's closing. It just feels like things are closing in. . . . There just seems to be a lot of stuff everywhere, whether it be heroes are falling down, people that you thought you could count on, you can't count on.

When the school culture itself was examined, it was generally not considered open to criticism. The students' unruly behavior, for example, could be explained as a normal result of the emotional comfort the school offered rather than as a vulnerability that might lead to fracture:

> I think that one of the things is that kids feel comfortable here . . . And this means that sometimes they don't have the curbs on their behavior, ah, that we would want . . . I'd say for most of our kids this is the most

stable part of their lives. And so, in a sense, we're not just teaching them math or humanities or creative writing, we're providing a lot of other things. Now, I, I think we need to keep talking about this and [keep] our priorities clear as possible and the boundaries as firm as possible. And you know, what systemically we can change.

The above statement interrupted the staff's potentially fracturing examination of the school's culture. This interruption, which framed the school culture as benign, held the vision of the school safe. It did not preclude an examination of the school culture but emphatically set that examination within a supportive context. The ways that the culture of this school supported student behavior and misbehavior had to be framed thus if they were to be successfully examined. The vulnerability such examination exposed, that perhaps undesirable student behaviors could result from the relatively safe haven constructed here, sometimes perplexed the staff to the point of pain. Yet the director's statement above demonstrated to the staff a tolerable interpretation of the realization that even the most conscientiously constructed curriculum and social environment will not produce docile and compliant students if student docility and compliance are not really desired by the community.

The Uptown staff considered the opportunity to have a voice in decisions to be essential to democratic decision-making (Calderwood, in press-a; Schwartz, 1990). They also stressed mutual respect and a willingness to accept responsibility and accountability for decisions made. According to the staff, collaborative staff decisions at this school were reached after long, sometimes exhausting, discussions. According to Vanderslice (1995), working cooperatively in groups can be a challenge even for the most dedicated. She notes that strong personal ties, such as those evident among this staff, "may foster . . . overtalking issues or decisions in an effort to please everyone and reach a true consensus. Overly long discussions can cause members to become frustrated and disenchanted with cooperation" (p. 183).

LEADERSHIP, AUTHORITY, AND ACCOUNTABILITY

Ideally, leadership needs a strong person. Then, there has to be community. The leader defines herself in strength which comes from the input of those in community. The bottom line is effective, honest communication. . . . Unless leadership is from community, with everybody feeling honored, feeling that they have real impact, and are essential, then you have the American dysfunctional family. There still is a sense that there is one person who is a leader. There are different leadership roles, and there needs to be someone to pull it all together.

Leadership is a community function. Uptown is a young community. It struggles with its lines of leadership and decision-making. It is still defining its process.

—Remarks made by an Uptown teacher

The management of consensus and democracy among staff in the three schools was largely the prerogative of the principals and director. Leadership and its prerogatives were not disputed at St. Margaret's Academy Elementary and High Schools. The staff in both schools accepted and validated the authority of the principals to make decisions. Dissent and consensus among the staff were largely irrelevant because the authority was clearly and uncompromisingly in the hands of their leaders, the principals. The burden of making responsible and wise decisions rested with these women, who consulted or not with the staff as they deemed necessary. Such streamlined authority and accountability were possible for various reasons, among them a fundamental core of values and beliefs, a clear distinction between appropriate spheres of authority and accountability among the staff and principals, a long tradition of hierarchical power relations, and the strong normative power of appropriate behavior.

The moral authority that is created and sustained by a school staff's consent to and validation of core values and beliefs belongs to the entire community but may become embodied in a leader, or in the role of leader (Bryk et al., 1993; Licata, Teddlie, & Greenfield, 1990; Sergiovanni, 1994). This embodiment of authority within a leader in no way diminishes the collective moral authority of the group. Rather, it is only legitimated if collective moral authority is sustained. However, when the fundamental core of values and beliefs is disputed, when members understand or articulate these differently, or when they cannot withstand challenge, this base of moral authority weakens, erodes, or may never even become established. Leadership may be compromised. The development of this moral authority is a delicate task even within a group committed to democracy (Sergiovanni, 1994). Vanderslice (1995) shows that cooperatives that do not have clear agreement about and commitment to the shared values around which they cooperate are more fragile and vulnerable than those that have clarity. "Members look to the organization's leadership to understand the particular meaning of cooperation in that setting. . . . It is essential for leaders of cooperatives to be able to clearly articulate and justify the values of their organization" (p. 194).

There was concern among some of the Uptown staff about a perceived lack of leadership by the director with regard to decision-making, as her indirect style indicated tensions between her preference for consensual decision-making and the realities of her individual responsibilities (Calderwood, in press-a). Although the director strove to keep many decisions in the power of the staff as a whole, she often had sole public accountability for many of the school's practices. It was imperative that any significant staff decisions that were made in the consensual arena be ones that she herself could support if pressed to do so (Licata et al., 1990; Vroom & Yetton, 1973; Yetton & Crawford, 1992). As a result of the director's dilemma, it was common for the staff to appear to drift into choices that would later be understood as moments within a particular decision-making process (Glasman, 1994). A lack of clarity, or failure on the staff's part to decisively resolve an issue that was ostensibly theirs to resolve, was a regular occurrence. It, in effect, freed them from accountability for consequences that followed from the choices made. This lack of clarity masked from the staff their actual abdication of the decision to the director or to a subgroup of the staff. The director, then, exerted her authority and made the decision by herself, or with confidantes and advisors, at least in some part on the basis of the staff's conversations about the matter.

The director believed strongly in collaborative decision-making but also needed to ensure, to the best of her ability, that the choices made were ones she could support. Her greater accountability demanded this. Presuming a consensual decision, even in the face of persistent dissension, made it possible to implement the plans she supported. Going through the process of "reaching a decision" with the staff was at times a process of her convincing them, wearing them down until they stop dissenting, overriding, ignoring, or not recognizing their dissent. Sometimes the process of "reaching a decision" with the staff required the staff to abdicate their decision-making responsibilities to the director.

The strength and fragility of community are both evident in the construction of leadership at Uptown. Because leadership was conferred upon the director by the staff, rather than existing as a given element of a hierarchical structure as it did in the two Catholic schools, the Uptown group made itself vulnerable to potential fracture from discordance. When the staff were at odds with each other, indirect consequences, such as contradictory carrying out of policy, sometimes resulted. However, the way that leadership was negotiated frequently strengthened community at Uptown. Each time the staff agreed to cooperate in the exercise of leadership, the feelings of being respectfully connected and mutually interdependent were raised, their professional identities were affirmed, and an example of what their community was about was created. Every exercise of leadership in this school required a conscious ratification by the staff that kept professional identity and feelings about professional identity clear. As the director became more comfortable with the authority of leadership, the opportunities for successful displays of her leadership increased, and the opportunities for fracturing discordance about how leadership should be constructed decreased. An Uptown teacher commented on the process:

"Director" is probably the most collaborative school leader that's out there. There is tension amongst staff because not everyone subscribes to a common plan of action. I think this is healthy. We are re-inventing school as we go along. We have a few models but mostly we're figuring out what we're doing as we go along. As long as we keep kids first and prioritize our plans based on their best interests I don't have a problem with accepting leadership from "Director." We need to function as a school. If there were no leadership there would be total chaos and anarchy. I don't think kids or teachers can learn in that kind of environment.

DIVISION OF STAFF RESPONSIBILITIES: CLARITY AND DISTANCE

At St. Margaret's Academy High School, the staff was departmentalized and compartmentalized (see Figure 3.1). This layering of the school's staff had implications for the nature of the staff–student social relations, leadership, and, consequently, the sense of community and interconnectedness that was available. The clearly demarcated roles of administration and teaching faculty were supported by extensive lists of rules and responsibilities, tight schedules, and prescribed curricula. When coupled with similar official rules for student behavior, as well as the unofficial student-designed codes of behavior, the organization of the staff and students generally was an impediment to the development of close and caring bonds between students and teachers. This distance was not considered a disadvantage by the adolescents or the adults in this school. It was considered appropriate.

The principal held the overall responsibility and authority for the operation of the school. According to the faculty handbook, she had "the ultimate responsibility and authority for the Christian orientation of the school and the fostering of the goals set." She was responsible for the hiring and supervision of the staff, supervision and coordination of the curriculum, public relations, finances, and student enrollment. The dean of studies organized academics. She was responsible for supervision of admission and graduation policies, the organization of individual student programs, testing and evaluation, report cards, student records, and so on. The dean of students organized the appropriate behavior of the students and staff. She had a long list of other specific responsibilities, including building-safety management, supervising the driver's education program, supervising assemblies, and so on.

Department chairs were responsible for communicating information from administration to the teaching staff. They planned the department's program of studies, electives, required courses, and the like. They supervised the de-

Figure 3.1. School organization at each site

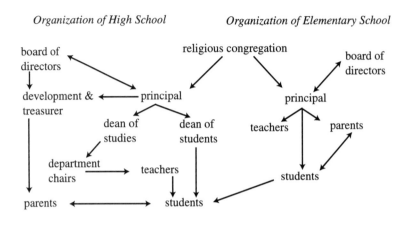

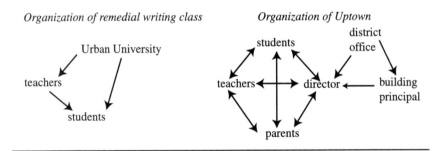

partmental budget, coordinated ordering and distribution of supplies, kept the staff up to date on methods, technology, information, and professional news, ran meetings, and so on. Teachers were responsible for classroom management, for guiding appropriate student behavior, and for enacting the philosophy and goals of the school in addition to instructing students in the academic subject areas.

The hierarchy of the high school staff was more complex and layered than that of the elementary school, Uptown, or the remedial writing class. At the elementary school, the administrative tasks of the principal, deans, and department chairs were carried out by the principal. Consequently, the elementary school principal's work was more visible to the teachers, students, and parents than that of the high school principal. At Uptown, the staff shared administrative tasks with the director. Necessary administrative tasks such as registration were handled by teachers and students in the remedial writing class as the need arose.

The layers of administration in the high school influenced the ways in which people interacted. The high school teachers needed to consider departmental and whole-school curriculum objectives and guidelines to a greater extent than did teachers at St. Margaret's Elementary School but to a much lesser extent than did teachers at Uptown. The high school teachers had little opportunity to individualize instruction for each student for two reasons. They did not have control of the curriculum, as did the Uptown teachers, and they did not have structured opportunities to form more than superficial personal relationships with the students.

Although the division of staff responsibilities might seem to indicate a separation of the academic, spiritual, social/emotional, and physical spheres in the high school, they did intersect. As is evident from the chart of the high school organization, no person worked in isolation, although there was not necessarily a direct line from one division to another. The dean of students, for example, ensured that the school environment was orderly and safe, an essential element to facilitate learning there. The dean of studies relied on this safety and orderliness factor when designing individual or school-wide programs.

Although some students saw the high school principal so infrequently that they did not recognize her when she observed their classes, her authority and leadership facilitated the effective management of the teaching and learning in the school.

GIRL TALK AND BOY TALK

A community that values its own diversity, as Uptown School does, must deal with the inevitable differences and potential tensions that arise in the balancing act of inclusion. The tasks are to understand how its community is supported and sustained by attending to the challenges of internal diversity, and to examine how this creates opportunities for fractures and for strengthening to occur within the community. This tension between strengthening and fracturing was always in play at the middle school, sometimes explicitly so and sometimes imperceptibly.

Elsewhere I have written of the trajectory of two classes I observed at Uptown School, Girl Talk and Boy Talk (Calderwood, 1998a). Practices of community were carried out differently in the classes. In contrast to the deliberately grade-, race-, and gender-balanced classes at the school, Girl Talk and Boy Talk were designed as classes where participation (or conversely, exclusion) was primarily determined by gender and secondarily by which students appeared to be in most urgent need of the class. Girl Talk and Boy Talk differed from each other in several ways, notably aim, pedagogy, and group dynamics, although there was considerable overlap in the topics discussed. Girl Talk offered time and space to examine and question the road map of being a girl. Boy Talk offered more practical information, a compass, so to speak, with which to navigate the road map of male adolescence. Some of the work undertaken in Girl Talk and Boy Talk exposed vulnerabilities within the school community, vulnerabilities that could create fissures or resilience, vulnerabilities that might undermine or support a vibrant sense of community. I concluded that the classes were perceived potentially to pose an intolerable level of fracture to the larger school community. In consequence, the way that students were selected for the classes and the paths of their participation changed, reducing the perceived threat to the well-being of community at Uptown. Let us look at a few moments of vulnerability brought to light by the students and teachers.

The Boys Talk

In Boy Talk, the teacher and boys read the American Association of University Women (AAUW) report, *Hostile Hallways,* a study of sexual harassment of students in high school (American Association of University Women Educational Foundation, 1993). The boys were surprised to learn that something they never really thought much about, calling other boys gay or fags, was harassment. Several of the boys discovered that they had harassed others, and two boys, with tears in their eyes, said that they guessed they had been harassed. "They call me gay," said Nelson. Ricky nodded, "Me too." The teacher asked them if they thought that other kids in the school needed to think about these things. He asked if they would like to replicate the survey at this school and compare their findings with those published in the report. The boys grew excited about this, especially about the suggestion that they could publish their results in the school newspaper. They made plans to type and distribute the surveys and agreed to conduct a simple analysis of the results. The idea of the boys' conducting such a survey was surprising and exciting because it challenged an assumption that the topic would have been more appropriate in the Girl Talk class, as the Girl Talk teacher had informally acquired a proprietary interest in the topic of "gendered issues." Sexual harassment was considered to fall within that category. However, the idea of boys examining the topic of sexual harassment was an affirmation that, in Uptown School, every member was committed to banishing sexist and other offensive patterns of behavior.

The teacher's decision to bring the report to the boys' attention made an uncomfortable vulnerability visible. One of the cherished images of communal relations held by the staff was that the school was a safe space for the students, a space within which the dangers of "outside" were held at bay and within which no student or teacher would cause harm to another. The students strongly desired to have this safe space and held the teachers strictly accountable for much of its maintenance. They were brutal in their critiques if the teachers erred, and this demanding stance was more pronounced among the older students than among the sixth graders. The teachers believed that they were successful in maintaining this safe space and regarded the absence of sexism and sexual harassment as a point of pride. The reality, and thus the vulnerability, was that the school was not as free from sexism, sexual harassment, and other related issues as the teachers and students would have liked it to be. That the boys and their male teacher wanted to carry out the surveys could have been seen, and to some extent was seen, as an indicator of commitment to the reality of the safe space, a celebration of the community's willingness to dispel danger and inequity from its interior. But what might the survey results reveal?

The surveys posed an opportunity for potential fracture to the larger school community. Misunderstandings, miscommunications, and misinterpretations were possible at every step of the process, and each was a potential point of fracture. Conversely, clear and accurate understandings, communications, and interpretations could also occasion fracture. A true picture might be reassuring to students and staff if it confirmed their cherished beliefs, but it might cause unbearable disappointment or unassuageable anger if the idealized vision of safe space did not hold true. Postponement of the surveys would provide time for reconsideration and possible redesign of the project, offering time to prepare buffers in case of disappointment or anger. Postponement would also prevent the surveys from ever being prepared and distributed, which is, in fact, what happened. As of the last week of school that year, the surveys had not taken place. However, the work of building buffers did go on. One element in the buffering was the staff's resolve to find out more about how to notice and deal more effectively with sexist patterns of behavior within the community; another was the staff's decision to become better educated about how to respond when they learned of any sexual abuse inflicted upon any of their students. The second resolution was made in the disturbing aftermath of a Girl Talk session in which many girls spoke about being abused.

The Girls Talk

Conversations in Girl Talk class also exposed vulnerabilities in Uptown community. The following excerpt is from my field notes during one of the last Girl Talk sessions of the first trimester:

Nina began talking about a new eighth grader. He is weird, she said. He worships the devil, he made inappropriate sexual comments, he has spoken of committing suicide. Nina feels afraid of him. Magdalena says, "So what if he worships the devil. That's no reason to be frightened. It's nobody's business what he believes." In response, the teacher stressed that tolerance for difference is, of course, desirable and just. But the boy had crossed a boundary and had invaded a space where Nina had previously felt safe. His offer to masturbate publicly for money offends and frightens. To tell another student that he often thinks of suicide is a terrifying act. The teacher posed questions: "How do we as a community become tolerant and welcoming enough to include the really different kids? How do we mark out the boundaries of inappropriate behavior?"

As noted earlier, the students counted on Uptown being a safe space for them. They wanted safety not only from "outside" but also from interior danger. The boy described by Nina acted in ways that frightened, disgusted, or alienated the girls in the group. His behavior was dangerous to them, they believed. Although agreeing that tolerance of the boy's oddities was a good idea, their teacher urged the girls to consider the ramifications of this tolerance on the well-being of the entire school community. She asked: "How do we as a community become tolerant and welcoming enough to include the really different kids? How do we mark out the boundaries of inappropriate behavior?" She explicitly invoked the importance of norms and boundaries within community (Cohen, 1985).

Although the students were not officially aware of it, the boy was one of the dozen MIS-1 students who had been admitted to the school that year. Like every child admitted to the school, he had participated in an interview with some of the staff as part of the admission process. The Girl Talk teacher told me privately that he had been admitted because the interviewers hoped that being mainstreamed at Uptown would be good for him. However, his needs and his behaviors were significantly different from those of most of the other children. He stood out, and his differences were disturbing. An area of community vulnerability became more visible because this boy had been admitted to the school. Were they prepared to teach this child and others who had such exceptional needs? Were the students willing and able to accept other students who acted oddly? Could the school community absorb such challenges to their behavioral norms without becoming fragmented? Offering Uptown as therapeutic to this boy resulted in other students feeling that they were in danger, that their needs for safety weren't being met. It also shook their confidence that they could really be in community, if they couldn't reach out to this boy in the ways that they valued and that they expected to work. It bothered the girls that they were deciding to reject the boy, to bar him from community.

When the teacher moved the Girl Talk discussion to the responsibility community members feel for each other's well-being, the girls saw, with her guidance, that it was not only possible but imperative that they demonstrate their responsibility to the boy and to themselves as a community by finding help for him. This moment of supportive community within the Girl Talk group transcended its own boundaries and was an affirmation of the resilience of larger community as well. The girls and teacher articulated elemental values of community at the school—caring about and supporting one another, tolerance and support of diversity and difference. They recognized how vulnerable their practices of community would be if they could not meet the challenge posed by the boy, and by other fragile students. The vulnerability itself remained within the practices of community, because there would still be students admitted to the school because someone judged that the school would be good for them, would help them overcome their troubles, and so on. Extraordinary as the staff was in its devotion to the students, however, they were not therapists, and some uncomfortably wondered if they were overreaching. It was difficult enough to be caring teachers who quietly and privately wrestled with how best to serve their students. The support of a climate that publicly criticized these difficult decisions undermined their confidence and sense of professional efficacy. Reducing the amount of public criticism would help keep the strain from spiraling out of control.

The School Responds

Other occasions of potential fractures to or support of resilient community abounded as the work of Girl Talk and Boy Talk progressed over the trimester. Beginning in October, a pattern of attempted interference with the classes emerged. Curious students and teachers found reasons to enter the classrooms while the groups were meeting. From mid-October through December, there was an increase in the number and the persistence of attempted interruptions of the Girl Talk class by other students, especially boys. In response, the girls began to lock the classroom door to ensure privacy. The Boy Talk group also began to seek more privacy. During the first half of the trimester, the boys and their teacher had been housed in the classroom of a female teacher, who generally remained in the room while they were in session. The boys complained, and eventually the class moved to a windowless storage room piled with boxes and supplies.

Interruptions became more insistent as time passed. With the consent of the faculty, remedial math classes were instituted during the middle of the trimester, and about a third of the Girl and Boy Talk students were compelled to attend, thus missing one of the two weekly sessions for the rest of

the trimester. Students were routinely pulled out of the classes, often to resolve disputes that had arisen during lunchtime. Trips and play practice interfered with attendance.

The consequent consistent absence of significant numbers of students
disrupted the developing and fragile sense of community that had been noted
by the girls as an important characteristic of their Girl Talk class. Early in
December the girls began one session by mourning the loss of their sense of
themselves as in community. "This class is dying," said Maria. The consistent
interrupting was a contributing factor to the loss of a similar sense of community in the Boy Talk class, although the organization of that class was probably a more important factor.

The potential for additional fractures of the fragile school community
seemed likely if the first trimester's class composition and organization stayed
the same, although the potential for affirmative strengthening of community
might have made tolerating these fractures worthwhile. The question of
whether the Girl Talk and Boy Talk classes might retain their current students
for at least one more trimester forced the staff to examine the relative merits
of "going deep" or "going wide" when the choice had to be made between
one or the other. As noted earlier, there were many students not currently in
either class who could benefit from them. A large number of students had
requested to be placed in the classes for the second trimester.

After weighing the pros and cons of continuing the classes with the same
or different students, the director of the school decided to repopulate them
with all new students for the second trimester, and again for the third trimester. The classes in the second and third trimesters had many more students
(28 rather than 16) than those in the first trimester. Also, more students from
sixth and seventh grades were enrolled in the classes than from eighth grade.
The eighth graders were enrolled in sex-education classes, which were taught
by different teachers. The younger students, according to the Girl Talk teacher,
were inexperienced at reflective critical analysis. The criteria for selecting students became more similar to those used for other elective classes. This time,
the classes did not have an exclusive cachet, nor were they composed of especially needy students. However, a few of the original students, deemed to be
still needy, were placed in Girl Talk for the third trimester.

Even though the trajectory of Girl Talk and Boy Talk was finite, it would
not necessarily have been concluded quite so early if left to evolve without the
outside interference described above (Rolston, D. C. personal communication, 1997). However, the scope and persistence of the interruptions were significant factors in the decision about how to continue the classes, for they were
a clear signal that what went on in the classes made outsiders feel uncomfortable or threatened. The best interest of the larger school community was a
necessary consideration. The discomfort caused by the classes' power to af-

fect the whole school was intolerable and demanded alleviation. The preclusion of the potential transformative changes that might have resulted from the maintenance of the original groups for one more trimester can be viewed simultaneously as a loss and as a benefit to the school as a whole. What good has been lost to the entire group, in terms of deepened and strengthened practices of community, can only be speculated upon, but the elimination of the discordance and discomfort caused by the unsettling activities of the classes was generally received with relief.

WHAT IS MADE OF DIFFERENCE AND DIVERSITY WITHIN COMMUNITY IS IMPORTANT

This chapter has shown that difference and diversity are attended to differently at the four sites and can be understood in multiple ways at any one site. What is consistent at all sites is that something, either significance or insignificance, is made of difference/diversity and that this treatment is closely related to the identity-making of the group. Let us return to the remedial writing class for one more example.

Sharon, the teacher of the writing class, routinely embellished the participants' comments, using them to foster a supportive sense of community in the face of that fearsome adversary, the Writing Assessment Test. In response to comments I had made to the class, she elaborated:

> You hear what I'm saying? All these things that we see in the movies and in the slick magazines aren't true. I got my first masters in 1963, and my second one in 1984, right, and struggling a decade, ten years, for a Ph.D. That's more like real life. *We're not the exceptions. That's what happens to real people, you understand.* The movies are not us. That's what you have to understand, it's like, you have to understand this. *You're not the exception, you're the rule.* And I'm saying this today—cause I want you. . . . You know what I'm about here, I'm devious, right? You've got to push, you've got to work hard. I've said this over and over in the years that I've known so many of you, right? And I've seen when people get low—we're human beings, right? It seems overwhelming. But if you quit this case, what are you gonna say to yourself ten years from now? I quit? What are you gonna say to your children? Mom and Dad quit? Hey, whatever will be will be, because you'll find other things to do. One thing you don't do is quit. So they put you out! Come back in a year! You know what I mean? Serious, right? Serious! Come back! It's only when you stop, you know? *There's things to do in life. You got to be willing to do it. All of you made a*

*choice to come here. We keep talking about it, right? And you know the
name of the game here, right?* The rules! Right? So the last 8 weeks
(cause next week is 8 weeks left, right?) you keep coming. You really
got to push.

The transformation of stigmatizing difference into shared honor was one
important goal of this conversation. The next step was the utilization of this
honor to support a determination to work to pass the writing test and prove
to the outsiders that these were indeed successful writers, not failures.

As has been shown in this chapter, internal difference and diversity were
attended to at each site. The idea that internal diversity is desirable was part of
the group sense of community at all four places, but the perceptions of what
counted as acceptable internal diversity and difference were not the same within
or across sites. At St. Margaret's Academy Elementary School, for example,
difference and diversity not attributable to personal effort were diminished or
ignored in order that the essential spiritual commonality could be cited. The
ninth graders at St. Margaret's Academy High School worked hard to ignore
diversity as they learned to fit into their new roles and identities. As we see in
the next chapter, differences such as having the wrong attitude were dangerous and to be avoided. At both Catholic schools, conformity and uniformity
were desirable attributes. They ignored, as much as possible, the kinds of difference and diversity that were celebrated at Uptown and in the remedial
writing class. As we see in the next chapter, learning to be always appropriate,
to always think, speak, and act in prescribed ways, was very important at both
of the Catholic schools. Much effort, on the parts of staff and students, was
expended to turn the students into good people who acted appropriately. This
appropriateness set them all apart from outsiders.

Certain kinds of difference and diversity were understood to be vital elements of community at Uptown school. The students, staff, and parents believed that respect and celebration of their differences and diversity was a central identifier of community there. Much was made of acknowledging and
striving to accommodate, in socially just ways, important differences such as
race, ethnicity, gender, and language. Less was made of the differences that
counted at St. Margaret's Academy Elementary School, such as honor-roll
grades. This celebration of internal diversity by taking care of individuals was
acted out in their attempts to root out internal inequities and injustices.

The acknowledgment of difference and diversity within the remedial
writing class was a painful and delicate experience. Because their differences
had been stigmatized so tragically by outsiders, it was necessary to use the
experience of stigmatized difference and diversity to build a new shared identity of struggling writers. Stigma became honor and pride and hope.

CHAPTER 4

Learning and Celebrating Community

Depending on the particular group, flexible or rigid norms of practice and corresponding flexibility or rigidity in the learning of these norms can contribute to the resilience of community. To illustrate, let us turn to several examples of how students and teachers teach and learn the ways of being in community for their particular groups. We will see that knowing how to be in community makes it possible to experience a sense of community or moments of communion. Closely tied in with the learning are the celebrations, some ritualized and some spontaneous, that contribute to the resilience of community.

LEARNING HOW TO BE A NINTH GRADER

During the first weeks of high school, the ninth graders at St. Margaret's Academy High School spent much energy on learning how to be a ninth grader in the ways that were acceptable at St. Margaret's. The very idea of being different was an intolerable thought for these students at this time of their lives. Isolation and estrangement were used by students as normative practices to ensure conformity of practice among the girls, in effect denying access to the comforting and stabilizing sense of being accepted into community. The fear of possible ostracism by other students was augmented by the desire to avoid punitive sanctioning such as poor grades for academic performance. The combination propelled many of the newcomers into achieving competence quickly.

Becoming competent in the practices of ninth grade was an arduous task even within the clear and inflexible parameters available. Consequently, the management of differences and diversity necessary to compose individuated and group identity as St. Margaret's ninth graders was fraught with vulnerabilities. Most of the attention to the vulnerabilities was undertaken willingly by the girls themselves. In addition to the self-regulation by the new students, the adults and older students in the school modeled and directly instructed the ninth graders in how to become more competent within community at St. Margaret's Academy High School. The comprehensive scope of the tutelage and learning indicates that this period of apprenticeship was of great importance, not only to the ninth graders but to the other community members as well.

Students Talk About Ninth Grade

The ninth graders began anticipating their apprenticeship within the high school community well before it began. I interviewed the eighth-grade class of St. Margaret's Academy Elementary School 3 weeks before their graduation in 1994. Of the class of 21 students, 13 said that they would be attending the Academy of St. Margaret's. They chose St. Margaret's because it was familiar, because it was so near their elementary school. They knew some of the students at the high school; some had sisters or mothers who had attended, and all knew the girls from the previous graduating class who had gone on to the high school. Continuity and familiarity offered comfort. The close friendships they had made in elementary school would continue through high school, and the 13 girls who would be attending the high school together would be able to count on each other.

They believed that the appropriate preparation for high school would have been high school itself. The students were nervous about their competence in a much larger setting than they had yet experienced. One girl comforted herself with the realization that all the other ninth graders would probably be new and scared as well. The girls wished that they had more practice in what they believed would be expected of them in high school, from academics and athletics to being able to find their way around the building to knowing how to get along with many new people. They were afraid that the high school teachers would expect and demand immediate competence in so many areas: academics, timeliness, finding classrooms, and so on. They were apprehensive about the new social skills they would have to develop immediately: getting along with many people, making new friends, going to dances and talking to boys, cheerleading, volleyball, play practice, organizing their time, looking good for school. It seemed exciting and, at the same time, overwhelming to the students.

In elementary school, the students were often told that things would be different in high school. The teachers regularly contrasted their own ways with those of high school teachers. When gently or not so gently chastising an unprepared student, teachers often mentioned that no high school teacher would be so lenient. The high school teachers would give instructions only once, and the students would be expected to comply. No excuses were acceptable in high school. The intentions of the teachers who made such comments were benign. They urged the students to become more responsible and more compliant, because those traits were highly valued in high school. They did not intend to plant the seeds of anxiety that sprouted in June of grade 8.

This anxiety about meeting their own expectations, coupled with the anxiety about meeting the expectations of their new teachers and older students, contributed to a hypersensitivity to norms and normative sanctions among the new ninth graders. They were eager apprentices, seeking to relieve their anxiety through successful assimilation into St. Margaret's.

In September and October 1994, I interviewed 10 of the 21 members of the 1994 St. Margaret's Academy Elementary School graduating class as well as 9 girls who had attended other elementary schools. In response to the questions, most of the students said that they expected to do well in high school, which to them meant getting good grades. However, some of the students were surprised by the difficulty of the academic work in high school, as evidenced by their test grades. They said they must work harder in order to maintain the grades they had earned in elementary school. One student said that she wanted to make the honor roll in high school, which had been unattainable for her in elementary school. She felt confident that she would be able to do so and attributed this to a combination of her personal growth and appropriate class placement. Students told me that the teachers expected them to pay attention, to keep up with the work, to ask questions, and to be prepared for class. One student believed that the teachers expected much more work from the honors students and also gave them more homework, and another expressed disappointment because the teachers promised to be understanding but were not.

The girls learned much about friendship in the first few weeks. Some learned that they were "unorganized," others that "it is hard to fit everything in and get it all done," and still others learned how to be responsible and independent. Few said that they had changed their ways of thinking, although one girl reported that she took studying and exams more seriously. The students survived with less sleep than ever, studied for longer periods, and no longer ate regularly. One girl, citing her tennis lessons, track team participation, and dance competitions, said that she had no time for herself. For some students, other changes included feeling pressured, rushed, and overwhelmed. A few students believed that they had more freedom now that they were in high school.

When asked how elementary school prepared them for high school, some of the students from elementary schools other than St. Margaret's cited frequent testing, much homework, strict discipline, and high expectations for academic achievement. Only one girl from St. Margaret's Elementary found her experience to be helpful in preparing for high school. She said that as a transfer student in grade 7 she had had to meet new people and adjust to a new environment. This had been good practice for adjusting to high school. Another girl from St. Margaret's discovered that she liked earth science class and wished that her elementary school science experiences had been better for her. She would have been placed into a Regents science class if she had learned more science in elementary school, she believed.

The honors students reported feeling overburdened for at least the first few weeks of ninth grade. Their schedules included an extra class, Latin I, every day. In addition to the extra course, the students were expected by their teachers and themselves to do more during class and for homework than the other students. Because they had been designated honors students by the school, the girls believed that they had little room to be less than completely competent. This meant that they had to manage to be timely with their class and homework assignments, carry overloaded book bags around all day, work through lunch, go to bed later and rise earlier than other students. In short, they felt they had to be working all the time.

Organizing Time and Space to Be a Ninth Grader

By mid-October, most of the girls in the honors class whom I followed from St. Margaret's Elementary School to the high school had found ways to manage their work loads, reduce their anxieties, and allow themselves time to relax. However, two girls were still struggling with the management of work. These girls excused themselves from being interviewed, although they were willing to chat during the 4 minutes between classes. Both said that they couldn't spare any of their free periods, which were completely devoted to doing homework, studying, and reading. In contrast, the girls I followed from the elementary school who were in Regents or non-Regents classes reported feeling comfortable with their work loads and schedules after the second week of school. They had more "frees" (times when no classes were scheduled) and felt less pressure to be perfect.

Most ninth-grade students had from 6 to 14 free periods per week, which were to be used to have lunch, to relax, and to study. The honors students had 10 "frees," or 2 each day during the first semester and 6 per week during the second semester. They were allowed, if they formally requested it of the dean of studies, to eat lunch during class on those days in which they had no other time set aside to eat lunch. The students in the non-Regents and Regents classes generally had enough "frees" available to devote at least one to studying and another to eating and relaxing each day. Some students, of course, did not use that time to study at all, and some students quickly gobbled their lunch while studying. The free periods were a particularly important part of the ninth graders' day or week. It was during these times that they learned and practiced a number of behaviors necessary for success—most important, how to get along with fellow students. The significant components of getting along, as some seniors, sophomores, and freshmen informed me, were being friendly and open, and developing the appropriate "attitude." Because most students chose to spend their free time in the cafeteria, the cafeteria became an important space in which to learn and practice how to be a successful ninth grader.

The students' time in the cafeteria, although nominally supervised by a teacher, was generally considered to be their own. There the students ate lunch, read, chatted, gossiped, listened to the jukebox, repaired makeup, wrote homework, or consulted with each other about schoolwork. The academic behaviors that took place in the cafeteria—doing homework, studying, and reading—were quite different from those in the library or in the classroom. They were generally accompanied by conversation about the next mixer, new music, or clothes, as well as by conversation that was more academic. More academic conversation might include cross-checking answers to homework questions, dictating homework answers to a friend, asking questions and offering ideas about topics studied in class, or examining specific incidents that had occurred in class. There were informal peer-tutoring and study groups that worked at test preparation. The rule was that there must be conversation rather than silence. It was also important to disguise serious academic pursuits by eating or drinking at the same time and by occasionally singing along with the music playing on the jukebox. It was not "cool" to sit apart from the other students and study silently. Students who needed to work differently found themselves in the library, where enforced silence was the rule. Although the students, particularly the honors students, professed that they wanted to do well academically, and did often spend at least some of their cafeteria time doing academic work, they quickly learned that they must balance this with other types of behavior. The balance was beneficial to the students. It provided a breather from study, which is hard work. It was an element of a structure easily discerned by the students, within which the girls increased their competence at being ninth graders. They practiced being friendly to their classmates, being deferential to the sophomores and juniors, and being worshipfully in awe of the seniors. They developed appropriate "attitude."

Appropriate Attitude

In June of their eighth-grade year, the transitioning students had told me about the importance of learning how to respect other people. Respect in high school, they quickly learned, included being appropriately deferential to sophomores and juniors, who described themselves to me as entirely deserving of this deference. A group of 10 sophomores said that the most important thing a new freshman had to learn was "not to have an attitude." Their postures, gestures, and tones of voice when speaking of attitude were markedly different from those of the freshman and seniors who also explained attitude. The overall tone when this group discussed attitude was characterized by suspicion, competitiveness, and hostility toward those who did not know how they should act. They confessed that they had had to learn these rules of attitude (deference to older students, minding one's own business, not bragging, etc.) themselves when they were ninth graders, and that it had been difficult, puzzling, and somewhat frightening to do so. Now, as competent sophomores, they were not inclined to be generous with the ninth graders. Their intolerance of attitude was accompanied by the powerful sanctions of derision and exclusion, contributing significantly to the anxiety of the ninth graders. Although the attitudes of this group seemed at odds with the prevailing norms, these girls powerfully reinforced the norms of compliance, sweetness, and consideration for others that were considered important elements of community at the school. In fact, experiencing the overt hostility of this group of students increased the desirability of the notion of a harmonious and loving St. Margaret's family for those unfortunate enough to have incurred its wrath.

When a quartet of senior girls was asked what the ninth graders needed to learn quickly in order to get along at St. Margaret's, their answers were quite different from those of the sophomores. They spoke of being friendly, of reaching out to make new friends, of demonstrating kindness. They advised the freshmen to be brave in this endeavor, because they remembered that it could seem scary at first. Good friends and wonderful friendships were invaluable and available. I asked them what "attitude" was. They listed arrogance, inconsiderateness, unfriendliness, hostility, being conceited, and having disrespect for others. They predicted that the current sophomores would eventually learn what was really important and jettison their current distorted attitudes.

The ninth graders were not certain that they knew what attitude was, but some were sure that they had somehow inadvertently violated a rule or two. One girl spoke of being pushed and challenged to a fight because she had brushed up against another girl accidentally. They all feared the animosity of the older girls.

During the first month of school, the ninth graders mixed caution with friendliness. They were careful to be considerate of other students, particularly when moving around the narrow, crowded corridors of the main school building. They modulated their gazes, their voices, and their body movements so as not to encroach upon the personal boundaries of other students. They began conversations with classmates as they walked through the corridors and often continued these conversations over lunch. They were deferential to sophomores and juniors but had little contact with seniors.

The 13 girls who had been together in St. Margaret's Academy Elementary School clustered together whenever they could. They maintained the close and familiar contact with each other that they had had in elementary school. Having each other for support was a great comfort in those first weeks of school. Although these girls did tend to group together during their free time, they began to include other girls in their groups immediately. The interviews that were conducted with the transition group would, often as not, include students who had gone to other elementary schools. When asked how they had become friends, the girls would generally reply that they sat together in class and had just begun talking about their assignments. Students from other elementary schools who were interviewed described the same process of making new friends, whether or not they belonged to a group of students from a single school. It was absolutely vital to have a cluster of friends for support, whether that cluster was composed of old friends, or girls recently met.

In St. Margaret's Elementary School, the girls had had little opportunity to be isolated or to form exclusive cliques. The school hadn't had enough students to support such cliques for any significant period of time. The small physical space made physical isolation impossible and conversational isolation difficult. The elementary school teachers would notice and intervene in arguments or estrangements among the students. The high school teachers, in contrast, had less opportunity to notice or intervene in such cases, unless these events interrupted class time. As the high school students had little opportunity to conspicuously interrupt classwork, few rifts among the students attracted the teachers' attention.

There were 114 ninth graders, almost five times as many classmates as the transition students had had in elementary school. For the first time, there was some variation in who one's classmates might be in different subjects. There was much more space for individuals and groups to separate from others. Formation of relatively impenetrable cliques became probable, as observations of older students at leisure indicated.

But in the early weeks of ninth grade, the groups formed and reconfigured as the students began to know each other better. During these first weeks, a ninth grader could make more choices about who might be her companions than could the sophomores or juniors. But she had to choose carefully if she wanted to become a successful St. Margaret's Academy ninth grader.

Jane's First Days in High School

Jane was one of the students who had come to St. Margaret's from the elementary school. She tested well enough on the placement test to be designated an honors student, and she was ever mindful of living up to the expectations (her own, her parents, and her teachers) this implied. Because her mother wanted her to experience "everything," Jane, by the end of September, had already gone on two optional school trips, tried out for the school play, continued Russian language lessons on Saturdays, and attended her first mixer. Jane had high academic expectations for herself but told me that it might take some time before her grades returned to the high level she had achieved in elementary school. She sometimes became confused among the three foreign languages she was studying: Russian, Spanish, and Latin.

Jane, friendly and personable, had a sunny smile, a delightful disposition, and a sweetly earnest manner in the classroom that her teachers found appropriate. She was strong enough to carry her heavy book bag without strain and agile enough to navigate her way quickly up and down stairs and from building to building. She was timely with her work, asked questions when she didn't understand a lesson, and performed well on tests. Perhaps most important, she was delighted to be a student at St. Margaret's Academy High School. A snapshot of Jane's first 2 hours of high school taken from my field notes follows:

Jane's first day of school was entirely taken up with freshman orientation. At 8:20 on September 7, 1994, she and several of her friends from elementary school were standing together in a crowd of about one hundred excited and nervous teenage girls. They wore casual clothing, obviously carefully chosen. A woman, later introduced as the director of development, was taking pictures of the students and striking up friendly conversations with them. She told them to look for the pictures on the bulletin board in the main floor corridor in a few days. At 8:40, the girls entered the cafeteria for orientation. When they were seated, the school's principal greeted them warmly. She addressed the group, repeating the advice the seniors told her to give, "Really enter into your years at St. Margaret's." Her goal for them, continued the principal, was to help them become "competent, earnest, deep-hearted young women." "Make friends," she urged them. "Be a friend. Join activities. Be earnest about schoolwork. Most important, be yourself." She challenged them to "Learn who you are and learn to be that person. Discover what you are good at."

The student council president bade the ninth graders welcome. Then the Dean of Students began talking to the girls. She spoke of high school as a time of opportunity. She bade the girls to choose to be happy, to join clubs, to be friendly.

The students were given their student handbooks, which are a combination calendar, date book, and source of rules and regulations. Then, the student council members conducted an ice-breaker activity, the purpose of which was to create groups of 8 to 10 freshmen and a senior. The groups chatted together, asking important questions. "Can you wear black jeans to school?" "When is the first mixer?" "What are the teachers like?" After about 15 minutes of conversation, the student council president addressed the entire class. She told them about the St. Margaret's tradition of big and little sisters. This would be an opportunity for the ninth graders to get to know someone older and, presumably, wiser in the ways of St. Margaret's High School, who would help them out and be nice to them. They would be matched up with their Junior big sisters the following week at a party. It would be lots of fun, promised the president.

The freshman were then introduced to the teachers. Then, the dean of students called out about 20 girls' names at a time. These were the homeroom groups. After each group was called, the girls and their homeroom teachers together walked across the campus to the main school building. They went to their homeroom classes.

In one homeroom class, two teachers and about 40 students faced each other. One of the teachers, a gentle-voiced Sister, began to explain some of the important things they would need to know right away. As she did so, she also took care to say that she knew that the girls were receiving an enormous amount of information today. She would not expect them to remember everything, but she wanted to address as much as possible this morning because she knew from her many years of experience that the students wanted to know everything right away. Her voice was slow, clear, and sounded very kind. She smiled reassuringly at the students and at her fellow homeroom teacher, a rookie. They would all get along just fine. The girls were told what the homeroom routine would be like. The students sat quietly, listening attentively. Nobody took written notes. Sister told them that the seniors who would be taking them around the school later would help them learn how to manage the lockers and the locks. "The seniors will help you out."

Sister gave out the schedules to the students. The students examined their schedules, and began to compare schedules with each other. The teachers stood quietly at the front of the room, smiling at the students. "We'll remind you about that again," said Sister after giving the students more information about schedules, uniforms, and so on. She told the girls that next Friday afternoon they would have their big/little sister party. Then she smiled broadly. "There's a mixer that night. Know what a mixer is?" The girls smiled back at her.

These notes about Jane's first 2 hours of high school demonstrate that much thought and preparation had been given to her and her classmates' successful initiation into the St. Margaret's community. The homeroom teacher's gentle and reassuring comments implicitly acknowledged the girls' apprehension and their desire to quickly learn how to become competent. She informed them of two celebratory events, the big/little sister party and the upcoming mixer, in which they would participate. Jane's eagerness to enter into competent community membership was supported by her fellow students and teachers because it contributed to the overall well-being and resilience of community at St. Margaret's. Her apprenticeship in community was under way.

During the days that followed, Jane and her fellow ninth graders were bombarded with explicit instructions from their teachers as they learned the routine of managing their academic work load. Although the teachers remained supportive, the tone had become much less warm and significantly more distant, as the following two examples from my field notes indicate. The speed with which this change took place, less than 2 weeks, indicates that the sense of urgency felt by the new ninth graders was not misplaced. They were indeed expected to become competent quickly.

> 9:59 A.M. biology. The teacher has taken attendance. "Tomorrow is the first lab," she says. "Choose a lab partner." As the teacher turns to write a homework assignment on the blackboard behind her desk, some of the students gesture and whisper to each other, setting up their partnerships. Then the students copy what the teacher has written into their student planners. The teacher turns on the overhead projector that is focused on the white screen pulled down over half the blackboard in the front of the room. She puts down a sheet of notes on the projector, and covers all but the first few lines. "I'll usually give notes on the overhead, because there are a lot of notes in biology. I will read them aloud to you," she stated. As she read the notes that outline the scientific method, revealing one line at a time, the students listened, viewed, and copied the notes into their notebooks. The teacher paused after reading each line, which gave the students time to finish writing. When she has finished this procedure with an entire sheet of notes, she looks at the students and asks if there are any questions. No student asks a question. Jane borrows a classmate's notebook for a moment. She compares notes in both books, in order to make sure that her own are complete.
>
> 11:30 A.M. Spanish. The thirty seated girls have just been handed some graded work by the teacher. She says that she will collect and grade homework from time to time. The girls will not know in advance when this will be done. The teacher walks around the room, textbook in hand, quizzing the students through a practice conversation.
>
> She tells them that spelling counts, in fact, that everything counts. Two students say that they did an assignment in a slightly different way than it had been assigned. The teacher tells them that they must translate exactly what she gives them. No substitutions are permissible, even if these substitutions make sense.

The work of becoming competent at being a ninth grader required intense engagement on the part of the student. Although the girls talked to each other frequently about what they were doing and how they were doing it, effectively cross-checking the appropriateness of their behaviors, these confirmation checks were seldom carried out in an atmosphere of calm reflection. Rather, they were urgent, frequent, and generally brief snippets of conversation that occurred while they were engaged in some other behavior, such as working on math problems, buying lunch, or rushing to class. This normative regulation was supplemented by the explicit, consistent, and patient instructions of the teachers regarding academic behaviors, official and informal rules for social behavior, and fierce monitoring by slightly more experienced students. The tightly woven network of explicit instruction by staff, successive approximations of appropriate behavior and attitude by the ninth graders, and the vigilant normative policing by older students ensured the transformation of the newcomers into competent community members. The rigorous attention paid to avoiding deviance from norms supported resilient, immutable community at St. Margaret's Academy High School. Once the ways of competence were learned by the ninth graders, explicit instruction tapered down, but normative sanctions, particularly concerning attitude, continued to be exercised vigilantly.

THE FICTION OF A NORMAL DAY

In a community that emphasizes commonality and behavioral conformity, being "normal" is important. At St. Margaret's Academy Elementary School, a standard response was offered each time I asked a teacher if I could observe the goings-on in his or her classroom. "It's not a normal day! We're testing, recovering from a test, doing a project, starting a new unit, planning the yearbook, going to Mass, leaving early, staying in for lunch, watching a video, just writing, just having a discussion, displaying our projects. . . ."

This fiction of a normal day served as a disclaimer: "We're usually more organized, well-behaved, productive, interesting. . . ." In addition, the fiction of a normal day served another important purpose for the teacher and students. Holding fast the idea that there is indeed a time when everything happens as planned, where learning and teaching are always optimized, where everything and everybody are entirely appropriate may make it tolerable to momentarily miss that goal. After all, usually the goal is met. Occasionally, toward the end of the second year of the project, some teachers would laugh and remark that I must think that there was no such thing as a normal day at St. Margaret's.

Because there is no "normal" day that can accurately be described, it may be useful to examine portions of a specific day in a specific grade, which can then be understood as a small part of the overall pattern of normalcy. For example, although tests are not administered every day, over the course of the school year it is normal to administer tests on a frequent basis. The interactions of the students and teacher on any given day are likely to resonate with the overall patterns of such activities. The aggregate of several years' worth of slightly deviant school days produces a pattern of normality against which radical deviations are easily noticed and explained. Acceptable norms of behavior are thus easily recognizable to teachers and students. Easily recognizable norms can be successfully internalized by students, through the process of successive approximations. The management of teaching and learning community norms then becomes routine and taken for granted as a result of such clarity. This is the way they do it here. The following snapshots from my field notes taken one early June day illustrate what, as I promised the fifth-grade teacher, will not be called a "normal" day.

The fifth-grade classroom is quite small, barely large enough to house the tablelike arrangement of student desks, a large teacher's desk, and two freestanding metal closets. As in every other classroom in the school, an American flag is secured to a small pole on the wall. Also, as in every other classroom, there is a shrine to Mary composed of a statue, a Bible, and some artificial flowers. Posters about grammar rules and the scientific method are on the wall. There are white writing boards on two walls, upon which the teacher and students write with magic markers. There are two doors to the classroom and one large window. A schedule is posted above the fifth-grade teacher's desk. It is one of the documents, along with the teacher's meticulously filled out plan book, that show how the school day for these students and their teacher is organized.

> 8:15 A.M. The students and staff are gathered in the cafeteria for morning meeting. As usual, the class sit together at a long table, excitedly chatting about television programs they have seen, what they did over the weekend, and so on. Today all 11 fifth graders (10 girls and 1 boy) are present. The girls are wearing their summer uniforms: pink seersucker skirts with short-sleeved white knit tops. As is usual, the students are seated by grades and the teachers stand nearby. The opening prayer, flag salute, and 5-minute information/entertainment program are orchestrated by another class today, so the fifth graders can relax. At 8:30 they walk together with their teacher to the building next door, ascend the single flight of stairs, enter the classroom, and unpack for the day. Notes and envelopes are given to the teacher, lunches and schoolbags are stowed, books and papers are crammed into desks.
>
> 9:30. Already, some of the children's shirts are untucked, some have ink stains on their hands, and ponytails are coming undone. Religion class is over, and the students are practicing long division with decimals. The teacher calls for volunteers to work a problem out at the board, and a number of students enthusiastically and noisily raise their hands to volunteer. After a girl is selected and begins working out the problem, the teacher interrupts the child's explanation of her work to comment on another student's behavior. "Stop that," she calls to the girl who has been playing with one of the many small personal items

that decorate the center of the students' table. As the teacher writes another problem on the board, the students chatter. Some of their talk is about social studies. The teacher hears them and tells them that now they are doing math. There are more long division problems assigned. As the students work, they talk to each other. The teacher shushes them. Realizing that they have been talking about the math problems, she apologizes. Math talk is okay during math class. At 9:55, it is time to get ready for French class, which is taught by another teacher, who waits quietly outside the door until invited in. The fifth-grade teacher takes paperwork across the hall to the staff room.

10:40. The students have finished French class and must now tackle spelling. They are told what to expect on their upcoming spelling test. As they puzzle over definitions, the students chat and laugh. One girl tells the researcher, "We laugh a lot!" However, the teacher finds the laughter inappropriate and calls for students to control themselves.

11:00 A.M. Test time. The teacher instructs the students to put away their books, and to take out rulers and pens. The students are moaning, "I hate tests." Instructions are given by the teacher. The teacher circulates among the children, who, one after the other, raise their hands seeking her attention. They ask questions about the test, a practice they have continued unchanged all year. Students read or do spelling assignments when they have finished. One girl who has finished begins telling an animated (though hushed) story about a cat and a bird to the teacher, who smiles as she listens. At 11:26, the last student finishes the test, and it is lunchtime. After the students have gathered up their jackets and lunches, they line up at the back door. With their teacher, they bless themselves and recite grace: "Bless us O Lord, and these thy gifts which we are about to receive from thy bounty, through Christ our Lord. Amen."

12:45. The students have been instructed by the teacher to open their reading workbooks to page 66. In response to a student's query, the teacher states that "We have a problem. We bring things up at the most inappropriate times." Just then, the second-grade teacher pops her head in through the back door. She comments on the students' sleepy faces. After she leaves, the teacher begins lecturing about reference materials. One girl balances a book on her head, an act that receives no comment from the teacher. This same student answers a teacher question with a long and very silly response.

Although the standard teacher disclaimer of abnormalcy was made, there was much about this day that was quite normal for the class. The students did chatter and laugh frequently, and were often silly. They struggled sometimes with math problems, with word meanings, with keeping themselves neat and clean. They worried about doing things properly during test time. They asked many questions of their teacher. The teacher was always well organized and prepared with her lessons. She consistently managed the students' behaviors and language. She determined what the official subject for consideration was at any time during the school day. They did take many tests. There was no individualized work, but a great deal of individual attention was given to each student. The teacher's insistence on denying the normalcy of this day was part of a general pattern of denial of the ordinariness of variation away from an idealized notion of St. Margaret's Academy Elementary School. A "normal" day for this fifth grade, or indeed for any other class in the school, had never occurred. Normal meant perfect adherence to the norms rather than more or less accurate approximation of the behaviors required by the norms. When the community participants are relatively inexpert, however, at understanding and adhering to the norms, as fifth graders often are, it is not possible to be perfect all the time. In addition, when the norms of a group cannot accommodate many of the real and persistently unique characteristics of the individuals who must be admitted into community, that group becomes vulnerable to fragmentation or dissolution. Thus the fiction is created and resolutely maintained that most of the time, normalcy is achieved. The energy that could be directed otherwise in attending to the potential vulnerability of not living up to the group ideal is spent maintaining the belief in this fiction, and in convincing others of its veracity.

Possibly because deviance from idealized classroom practice can generally be justified as pedagogically appropriate when it occurs, there is little danger that, when viewed as only occasionally present, such deviation is a significant vulnerability. Why, then, did the teachers at St. Margaret's consistently remind me that "today is not a normal day"? Perhaps it was an artifact of the strong normative thrust of community here, a thrust that did carry more urgency in other manifestations of deviance from conformity to the group norms that supported its identity.

LEARNING HOW TO BE GOOD AND APPROPRIATE

The ways that people learn how to think, speak, and act acceptably within community are many. In functional communities especially, as explained earlier, it is of great importance that community norms are well learned and conscientiously maintained. Consistency about expectations is paramount. Rigorous policing of how well group members adhere to the norms is practiced in functional communities, as we saw in St. Margaret's Academy High School, but would be impossible to carry out if allowances were not made for the novice to move toward adherence through successive approximations guided by direct and explicit instruction. This accommodation is well established in St. Margaret's Academy Elementary School.

There is a built-in time table for paths to maturation in skill and knowledge in schools (see Figure 4.1). In St. Margaret's Academy Elementary School, there were clearly marked paths to such maturation. Labels for community norms of behavior are used to call up and mark out the norms. The labels of *good* and *unacceptable, appropriate* and *inappropriate* were used at St. Margaret's Academy Elementary School to do this work (Blot & Calderwood, 1995). In fact, the school's success in maintaining community norms can in large part be measured by the aggregate appropriateness of its members.

Every student was expected to eventually learn how to judge what is appropriate, and to modify her behavior to remain or become appropriate. However, the young children were not asked to differentiate between appropriate and inappropriate behavior but were instructed about what behaviors, values, and beliefs were good or unacceptable. There were numerous opportunities to learn how to be good, either through explicit direction of behavior or modeling by teachers and more experienced students. Good behavior was frequently rewarded with subtle or exaggerated approval by the teachers, with words that often emphasized connection, caring, and respect. Such reward implicitly and explicitly evoked a sense of being in harmonious community.

In contrast to learning the differences between appropriate and inappropriate behavior, using one's judgment to discern the nuances of goodness versus unacceptability in dress, language, behavior, beliefs, and so on, was unnecessary. If a child did something unacceptable, she was publicly reprimanded. This provided an opportunity for the individual and the group to have a specific incident illustrate and be linked with a specific label, making the norms of community clear and simple to learn.

Figure 4.1. Learning to be good and appropriate at St. Margaret's Academy Elementary School

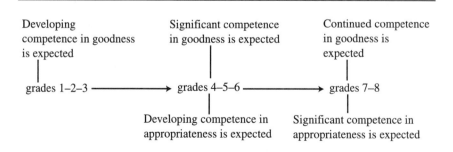

The public reprimands did not have to occur frequently as long as they were powerful. For example, one day in April, a first grader did not do her math homework. She confessed this to the teacher as the class prepared to correct their homework. In response, the teacher told her that this was "absolutely unacceptable," especially as this was not the first such occurrence. Clear and immediate actions to be taken were enumerated. The child could not participate in the next lesson, she was to complete the homework at lunchtime instead of taking recess, and she was to be sure to have all her future homework completed as assigned.

This interaction was a public event within the first-grade classroom. The other girls and boys quietly watched and listened to the drama, then set to work with elaborate industry. The incident was managed by the teacher to ensure that the singled-out child could not seek or receive any comfort, expression of care, or sign of solidarity from the other students. She was effectively, if only briefly, cast aside and scapegoated. The blame for the fracture in student solidarity was laid on the offending student rather than on the powerful teacher. The lesson learned by the students, who might have secretly pitied the outcast, was not to do what she had done—they must strive to be good. Being good promoted a sense of community, whereas acting in unacceptable ways resulted in the temporary loss of communal connections in addition to humiliation and other negative consequences. The norm of acceptable behavior within community in this classroom and the school was affirmed and reinforced by the punishment for the unacceptable deviation. The first-grade children's pain of existing with an outcast in their midst was considered tolerable in light of the bolstering affirmation of what is good and acceptable for the common good of the larger community.

After the homework had been corrected and the students had started another task, the teacher explained her behavior and frustration to me. She reported that the child was often in the care of her grandparents, as her mother was a single parent who worked long hours. The grandparents did not always make sure that the child's homework was done as the teacher expected. The message was that "inappropriate" behaviors by the adults in the child's life contributed to the unacceptable behavior of the child. The model of a good family was given as that enjoyed by another student in the class, who was one of four children in a traditional nuclear family parented by a hardworking and devoted homemaker mother and breadwinner father. Her descriptions of good and inappropriate families echoed staff-room discussions about diverse family configurations, differing values, and the effect of these on students' academic and social behaviors. Coleman and Hoffer (1987) discuss family configurations, using labels such as *disadvantaged* and *deficient*, in their analysis of variations in the social capital of families. At St. Margaret's Academy Elementary School, there seemed to be greater tolerance for and acceptance of families regarded as disadvantaged (for example, by poverty or institutionalized racism) than for families seen as deficient (for example, single-parent families or those where parents were too busy). Deficient families were inappropriate, and unacceptable behavior flourished in "inappropriately" configured families. It was most urgent that students from such inappropriate or unacceptable families be rigorously trained at school in acceptable and appropriate behaviors. The threat of potential deviation from the community norms was strong for those students whose families did not conform.

By about the fifth grade, the students had been extensively trained and had evolved into good students, a highly salient component of being good, as Purpel (1989) and McLaren (1986) have also noted. They strove to please their teacher and seldom did anything unacceptable. However, they could still act inappropriately. I observed a number of test-taking events in the fifth-grade classroom. Each time, the students, eager to please their teacher and to do well on the test, which during testing is the same thing, sought reassurances, explanations, or reiterations. They wanted to be sure that they knew what to do, what a test item meant, what the procedure was, and so on. The teacher responded to these requests patiently at the beginning of the year, and with occasional sighs and noticeable irritation as the pattern continued through the year. She told me that this was exasperating because it was inappropriate. She expected them to know what to do without the need for her to repeat the same information every time a test was given. By fifth grade, the students' significant competence in being good community members was considered developmentally appropriate, and normative processes toward students' development of appropriate behavior were undertaken by the teachers. Just as they had learned good behavior, students were expected to learn how to be appropriate through direct instruction and through modeling.

By grades 7 and 8, the students were expected to learn to distinguish between appropriate and inappropriate behavior. The previously mastered categories of good and unacceptable provided a foundation for and were encompassed by the emerging categories of appropriate and inappropriate. Although mastery of appropriate and inappropriate behaviors was expected by grade 8, sixth graders were supported with direct instruction about appropriate behavior. An example illustrates.

One muddy March day, several of the eighth graders began a verbal argument during lunch hour that rapidly deteriorated into a food- and mud-slinging event in the schoolyard. The sixth-grade class was present, and some students witnessed the fight. The principal spoke to the sixth graders about the "inappropriate behavior" they had witnessed.

It is shortly after lunch, about 1:00 P.M. The sixth grade students, all girls, are playing basketball under the direction of the gym teacher. The school principal enters the gym. She needs to talk to the students now. She looks distressed. Her voice quavers as she searches for the words she wants to say: "I just need you to know, um, I don't know what you know about something that happened outside that was inappropriate behavior. But, just be aware that any behavior that you observed that was very inappropriate was just that—inappropriate. And the fact that you see anyone else acting inappropriately should tell you one thing, and one thing only. That if it's inappropriate, you are not going to do it. Okay? And you know that here at St. Margaret's, we do not throw things at each other. Right? . . . Anything you observed out in the schoolyard, it has been taken care of and it was inappropriate. And I do not wish that you would get involved in that, this year, next year, or in eighth grade. If you know what I'm talking about, fine. If you don't, just take the words that I'm saying and remember them. If ever you're in a situation where something just doesn't seem right, just don't get involved. No matter what it is. Just go in the other direction. Okay?"

She left the students sitting on the gym floor, big-eyed and quiet. It was not clear that they all knew what she was talking about, but her distress was obvious. These good girls were moved by the principal's obvious pain. Although the norms of appropriate and inappropriate behavior were explicitly addressed, other norms were also modeled for the children. Compassion and caring were modeled by the principal and reciprocated by the girls. The feelings of compassion connected the group of children and adults and facilitated the interiorization of the lesson about appropriate behavior. The vulnerability exposed by the shocking deviation from the idealized norm of always appropriate student behaviors was alarming, and measures were quickly and briefly taken to diminish its power to fragment community. Dwelling for any extended period of time on the food fight could have led to questions about why it had happened. Answering that question honestly, as we see later, would have exposed the community norms as unrealizable fictions. This would have been intolerable. Had such an event happened at Uptown, in contrast, the entire school would have, in one fashion or another, exhaustively examined the question of why the fight had happened. There, the notion that problems cannot be hidden away, no matter the risk to sense of community and community identity, was more important than maintaining a fiction of harmony.

Tradition and Appropriate Behavior

The work of making students appropriate continued in St. Margaret's Academy High School, although the ways available to teach and learn appropriate community behavior were distinct from those of the elementary school. The notion of family and of coming home to school or to work became more important, as did the notion of tradition. The staff, particularly those who had attended the school as students, had a point of reference and comparison between "the old days" and the present. Continuing the traditions of the school bolstered the solidity of community here. Making generation after generation of happy, successful, and appropriate St. Margaret's girls gave a sense of strength and continuity to the St. Margaret's community.

The staff's work to instill "appropriate behavior" in the school's current students was often referenced to memories of appropriate student behavior in the past. Their values and appropriate behaviors were considered by insiders to be timeless and classic. Respect for authority, acceptance of responsibility, appropriate language use, manner of dress, timeliness, and so on, were to be carried out in the St. Margaret's way.

Although the notion of the good old days when students knew how to behave appropriately without explicit instruction from the staff was invoked regularly, it was understood to be fictive. As the principal reminded the dean of students, students misbehaved when they themselves were in high school. Gum chewing, for example, was always in dispute. However, according to the dean of students, there was more alignment of home values, general societal values, and school values in the good old days. Students did not use foul language so casually then, and they were more deferential to their teachers then because they had learned this behavior at home.

As at the elementary school, not every student who attended the high school had learned appropriate behavior at home, because, as the dean of students stated, general societal norms have changed, eroded, or relaxed. Therefore, it was the responsibility of the school staff to explicitly teach St. Margaret's ways to the students. Emphasis in the school was not on placing blame for these shortcomings but rather on effectively, firmly, and lovingly shaping the students' behaviors and values. The staff believed that the students were generally comfortable with the school guidelines because these were reasonable, fairly administered, and explicit.

This clarity and certainty supported the staff's sense of professional identity and their sense of loyalty to community here. The certainty of knowing exactly how to contribute to the current and future development, well-being, and success of the students was a dominant feeling among the teachers. The central values and acceptable practices here were sturdy, shining with the polish of generations of devotion. Like the Uptown staff, the staff at St. Margaret's Academy High School believed they were doing what was right for their students. However, unlike at Uptown, here the staff's concern was to shape the students to conform to the long-established tradition of St. Margaret's identity. At Uptown, the staff's concern was to shape the school climate to be responsive to the needs of the students. Students conformed to expectations at

St. Margaret's, whereas Uptown changed in response to the needs of the students. In both schools, the professional identity of the staff was tied to the behavior of the students, but the nature of this relationship differed.

It was seen by the staff as their responsibility and their gift to the students to guide them in appropriate behaviors. This was understood by the staff to approximate and prepare the students for the appropriate behavior expected in college, business, professions, and mature personal relationships. Students, whether or not they shared the belief that the St. Margaret's version of appropriate behavior was beneficial to them, generally accepted and abided by the explicit guidelines they received daily from the staff. As was evident from the description of becoming a ninth grader, the students had additional guidelines or rules about appropriate behavior that they themselves constructed.

There was little conflict in the observable behaviors of students who followed the official and informal staff-given guidelines along with the unofficial ones that came from students. The underlying values and beliefs sometimes differed in the two realms, yet still influenced the enactment of compatible behaviors.

A committee of teachers and the dean of students, which called itself the appropriate behavior committee, developed an explicit set of guidelines for appropriate student behavior during September 1994. This committee was formed during the first staff meeting at the suggestion of the dean of students, who believed that this would be a preventative step that would set the desired tone for appropriate behavior early in the school year. It was important to do so because the behavior of some of the students and faculty the previous year had not been appropriate. Students had been using foul language, or wearing caps, for example, and some faculty members had been tolerating such deviations. Some teachers had been drinking coffee in their classrooms, thus setting an inappropriate example for students. It was agreed by the committee that these guidelines would be read over the public address system during homeroom, one or two per week, or as deemed necessary. It was also agreed that the staff would consider itself bound by these guidelines as well. As the dean of students pointed out, it would be hypocritical, unfair, and oppressive to impose more stringent standards of behavior on the students than on the staff.

A point of interest is that the guidelines did not merely point out appropriate behavior but delineated unacceptable behavior. Unlike the older elementary school students, the high school students sometimes did act in unacceptable ways, necessitating the maintenance of strong normative measures to reduce such behavior. As in the elementary school, students who engaged in inappropriate behavior received remediation, whereas students who engaged in unacceptable behavior were subject to other disciplinary consequences, such as detention or parental notification. As we have seen in the elementary school, good judgment was needed to determine appropriate behavior, but unacceptable behavior was clearly marked and not much subject to negotiation. The rigidity of the norms concerning unacceptable behavior was important to the general health of the community, whereas the relative leniency regarding inappropriate behavior provided necessary opportunities for the students to continue their development of sound judgment.

Care was taken by the committee to limit the rules to those seen as absolutely necessary, but only because the dean of students persuasively argued that the students needed opportunities to choose and practice appropriate behavior without coercion, and that it would be counterproductive to overlegislate or to severely restrict their ability to practice self-control. She played the role of advocate of students' rights as strongly as she did the role of rightful authority over their behavioral boundaries. She was a conscientious arbiter of the appropriate balance between student rights and teacher authority—moderating both for the common good of school-wide harmony. The acceptance by all of her moral authority to carry out this role indicated strong value agreement about the rules and norms she oversaw. The way she carried out her role provided space to heal the small fractures to community togetherness inflicted by student–teacher power struggles, intrastudent discord, and other threats to school harmony.

The balance between individual needs and communal well-being was not difficult to manage at the high school owing to a number of factors, including the value place on conformity and an accompanying devotion to tradition. In a school with newly established traditions and flexible norms of behavior, however, the art of balancing individual and communal well-being becomes more artful and more challenging.

THE DELICATE BALANCE AT UPTOWN

A challenge at Uptown was to understand in what ways its community was supported and sustained by attending to the specific needs of individual students and by examining how this focus created opportunities for fractures and for strengthening to occur within the community. One painful example, an epidemic of thefts in the 1993–94 academic year, illustrates the delicate balancing act that took place as the staff sought to repair damage to the entire school's sense of trust in each other as the thefts continued over the months. Experience indicated to the staff that it was likely that the thefts were the actions of one or a very few students, and this was discovered to be the case. However, no public discussion of the discovery of the identity of the student was conducted, because the staff agreed that that would have had a devastating effect on the child, and possibly on the entire community. In consequence, the students never received satisfactory reassurance from the staff that the epidemic was treated appropriately. A result, as evidenced by the student surveys, was some pervasive feeling of mistrust. The quiet outcome was that one troubled student received some much needed help. The staff chose to tolerate a fracturing of school-wide trust, and the choice was bolstered by the knowledge that fractures can heal.

The middle school students and staff held expectations that the faculty and other staff members would make sure that Uptown was a generally safe place. But they also held expectations that the faculty would be sensitive and compassionate when individual students were troubled. In order to meet the second condition in this case, the staff could not bring public closure to the epidemic of thefts. The generalized anxiety that was a response to the thefts gradually faded away, although leaving a residue of doubt among the children that the staff really could keep them as safe from harm as they expected. An incident that occurred the previous year had already laid a foundation for such doubt. In this earlier case, sixth-grade students were kept in class and searched immediately after a single theft had been reported. The students were outraged about the violation of their expectations for sensitivity. That event was cited by several students during interviews carried out by one of my colleagues and during discussions about justice carried out in the research course she and I taught. The criticism of how the previous year's singular theft had been handled certainly influenced the more sensitive approach taken during the epidemic of thefts.

In a school where trust and safety are of paramount concern, how such incidents are handled is of more concern to the robustness of community than the thefts themselves. In the aftermath of the epidemic, the staff acted to reestablish a sense of security and to maintain trusting relations but could not receive credit for this because of the need to protect the child's privacy. However, the way the staff acted to solve the epidemic increased their own sense of competence and professionalism and was an opportunity to practice resilience. In the earlier, singular episode of theft, trust suffered because the students felt violated. That incident, however, brought some sense of shame to the staff, although this sense of shame did not increase the fragility of the social relations of community. It was transformed into a commitment to act more sensitively in the future. It was a catalyst for additional opportunities for professionalism to grow among the staff. Admitting to poor decisions, examining them, setting policy to ensure more sensitive responses to similar problems, and carrying out the more sensitive policies are practices of resilience here.

Recall the earlier described food fight at St. Margaret's Academy Elementary School. The response to the disturbing incident was swift. When the principal spoke to the sixth graders, she indicated how they were to understand and respond to what they had seen, and also how they should respond if they ever witnessed such behavior again. The principal spoke to the witnesses so that they would understand that what had happened among the eighth graders was a violation of the school ethos and was not to be seen as normal. Her purpose included the reassurance that the school was a safe place but, more important, placed the responsibility for maintaining that safety with the students rather than with the staff. The students were expected to know how to act appropriately, and this appropriate behavior was to be firmly grounded in the respect and fellowship that result from membership in a spiritual family. The sixth graders mostly seemed baffled by the principal's response, neither dissatisfied nor particularly reassured that they would be safe from witnessing such events again. There was no ripple of distrust, no fracture to their sense of community expressed. After the principal had addressed the sixth graders, she explained her speech to me.

Principal: They threw food and mud at each other outside.

Calderwood: It was all the eighth graders?

Principal: Just six. But it was in reaction to each other. And, a sixth grader had a yogurt pie, and it was their pie that was thrown around too. I think. Some of them saw it and some of them didn't. You could tell, some of them were looking at me . . . and I don't want to be specific because, you know, they didn't see it.

Calderwood: That's really a shame.

Principal: Well, it's a shame that they don't know how to make a mistake and admit their mistake and then let it go. They can't handle being wrong. They're very competitive, they work really hard to get good grades. They have poor self images, they don't. . . . It's something that some of them have grown up with. It's an offshoot of maybe, I don't really know what background, I'm not sure what background. It's sort of the emphasis they put . . . it's excuse upon excuse upon excuse. And it's usually, the excuse is outside. They spend so much energy on all of the excuses instead of saying okay, I'm gonna learn to recognize the signals next time and go in the other direction, turn my back. They got angry with each other and they just lost their heads for a second.

Later conversations with the eighth graders indicated dissatisfaction on their part with how this was handled; they believed that more serious punishments should have been meted out to the perpetrators. This was a very disturbing event for them, in part because it revealed the fragile, tenuous connections among this eighth-grade class. The impact of the food fight was damaging to their collective sense of being in community, which had never been secure, and which, in a few months, would become only a memory.

They also believed that there were serious and disturbing underlying issues that caused the fight, which were not addressed at all. The girls, as young adolescents are wont to do, were critiquing an apparent discrepancy between the principal's practice and the values she espoused. The students expected or hoped that these deeper issues to which they alluded—jealousy, competition, and hurtful gossip—would be resolved or at least explicitly addressed. When they were not addressed explicitly, the girls decided that the principal was negligent of her responsibility. They thought that she was acting inappropriately.

This fight greatly distressed the principal. Her distress was not limited to the fact that the students were bickering. She told me that she was aware of the tensions among the class members and had some understanding of their root causes. She felt that there was a great deal of competition for grades and favors among the students that was directly related to the stresses their families put on achievement. In addition, the principal believed that such pressure disabled the students from recognizing and owning up to their mistakes or inadequacies. They did not display the compassion and tolerance for each other that could have precluded the unpleasant incident. She chastised the girls for their behavior but did not punish them. Her behavior actually was in total accord with her values of compassion and tolerance and did meet the standard for appropriate behavior. She felt compassion for these girls who did not appear to be able to enter fully into a sense of community with each other. However, she would not allow their misfortune to spill out and infect the rest of the school. She exercised her leadership and authority to limit any potential damage to the school.

The students wanted clear and uncomplicated rules and categories presented to them, with immediate and just consequences. The principal expected them to be competent enough to maintain appropriate behavior and to interrupt any inappropriate behavior early. Because their fight indicated that they were not yet competent, the principal provided the students with explicit information intended to increase their competence at appropriate behavior. Punishment would have been an inappropriate consequence, and would have been in conflict with the values she wanted the girls to embrace.

Like the Uptown students, however, the eighth graders at St. Margaret's expected more than compassionate understanding that there were problems among them. They wanted the faculty to protect them by attending to the underlying discord that prompted the food fight. What they received, however, was a firm compassion expressed as exhortation to gain competence in behaving more appropriately. Self-discipline was to be practiced as the way to overcome underlying problems. The eighth graders were very dissatisfied, but their discontent and discord were not seen as evidence of fracture to the whole community by anyone other than themselves. The staff was just waiting for them to graduate and leave the school community in its normal state of peace. Discord did not offer the opportunity to transform vulnerability and its potential fractures into resilience. This discord was seen as an uncomfortable aberration, and its source was located outside the school community. There was something about the girls' families, about their inability to accept mistakes, about their excessive competitiveness, that fueled the problem. The school community was not flawed, the underlying discord was not threatening when it was contained within the confines of the eighth-grade classroom. However, it did become threatening once it spilled out to be witnessed by the sixth graders. Hence the immediate response by the principal that labeled the food fight as an unfortunate aberration.

Locating the roots of student behavioral problems outside the school culture accomplished similarly important ends at Uptown and at St. Margaret's. In both schools, a compassionate wisdom helped shape a manageable psychological profile of the students, a profile that guided adult responses to the students. Individual psychological profiling was much easier to manage than a comprehensive cultural analysis of how undesirable behaviors were supported in the schools, not because the adults were unwilling to accept their fair share of accountability but rather because psychological profiling did not threaten their idealized visions of how community was practiced. Maintaining their faith in their practices affirmed their sense of community and allowed them to act in ways that preserved community while attending to the students' needs. Attributing the vulnerabilities presented by undesirable actions of students to their individual psychological factors was generally a course of action that averted potential fractures.

Although the food fight did not present an opportunity to solve the eighth graders' real problems, it did offer the opportunity to affirm community norms that ensured appropriate behavior. The strength of disapproval was enough of a sanction to ensure that this would be an isolated event. The strength of the normative power of community absorbed the insult to its sense of propriety. Is this resilience? Perhaps, if resilience is considered the ability to continue on undamaged and unchanged. Perhaps not, if resilience is an outcome of the opportunity to grow in the ability to adapt successfully to challenges and vulnerabilities. At Uptown School, adaptive resilience is more salient than at St. Margaret's, where insusceptibility to vulnerability or fracture is valued.

COMMUNITY IS USED THERAPEUTICALLY

The notion of the therapeutic function of community follows from the work of Bellah et al. (1985) in their widely read book, *Habits Of The Heart: Individualism and Commitment in American Life*, in which the therapeutic benefits of a communal orientation in one's life are suggested as desirable and necessary for all people. This is distinct from the medical model of therapeutic community (for example, a mental hospital setting or substance abuse facility), which is seen as a holistic intervention that sets those diagnosed as severely damaged aside from "normal" healthy folks in an attempt to retrain them to be more "normal" and healthy. Those who call for what I label "therapeutic injections of community" are, in general, in agreement with the philosophy of Bellah and his colleagues and are not asking for medical interventions. However, a thorough analysis would not support such a clear demarcation, for each builds upon an implicit model of desirable and healthy norms of personal development, although the prescriptives differ significantly.

In the survey given to the Uptown staff in the fall of 1993, the staff had been asked to respond in writing to the statement "The school is a therapeutic community." I included this statement because its utility and accuracy as a descriptor, although hotly disputed by some powerful participants, continued to interest me as a possible way to understand some of the practices I observed. The exploration of the staff's understandings of how the process of community was used beneficently and therapeutically to benefit the students (and parents and staff as well) provides some useful understandings of how the fit between practices and their possible meanings is negotiated.

Although the notion of a nurturing, healing, healthy climate was a cherished ideal toward which the staff aspired, and although many of their practices, from the outside perspective, were centered upon strengthening a student's psychological and physical well-being, the staff primarily viewed themselves as educators, not therapists. However, the understanding of the roles and responsibilities of educators was not limited to teaching mathematics or humanities but also included, for every staff member, attending to the specific individual circumstances of a student's life that interfered with or supported his or her academic development. As many of the students were burdened with the gamut of complications that poverty brings in addition to their important work of adolescent development, some had to meet numerous obstacles before they could successfully attend to academics. Thus these responsible educators acted to help the students negotiate their way through or around these obstacles so that they could then attend to their studies.

The staff used every resource available to assist their troubled students. Sometimes they worked through academic channels, such as explicitly teaching study skills, providing tutoring, giving out notebooks and pencils, and badgering students about overdue work. Other times, this academic focus was not sufficient. The hungry child needed a meal, the anxious child needed reassurance, the lonely child needed a friend. Less often, but still regularly, children or their families required medical and legal assistance, formal counseling, and so on. As discreetly as possible, these needs were also addressed. One teacher wrote:

I think it is therapeutic in that we consider very seriously where a kid is coming from—their motives, needs, emotions created by their psychology. I also think it is because we try to work with a kid's emotions and feelings, to deal with their needs, to help them figure out what's going on for them. There is a lot of discussion and analysis. I think the staff is justifiably weary of being too involved and too therapeutic—of stepping over a line—of violating boundaries.

When we look at the school as if it were a therapeutic community, with some of the students in need of rescue from their various difficulties, the staff members become therapeutic agents of rescue. This resonates with the definition of their group as one in which everybody's needs are attended to. In this school the staff spends much time individually and collectively doing this work. Teachers who cannot, or who are not willing, to undertake this work are not Uptown teachers. Ordinary, outsider teachers cannot or will not do this work to the extent it is expected at Uptown. Such ordinary teachers are not very well regarded, nor are they welcomed into the group by the Uptown staff, students, and parents.

There is a tension made evident when the staff acts to change student attitudes—one that reveals a fragility in intergroup relations among the participants that is tolerated because the work is deemed essential to the well-being of individuals and, consequently, the entire community. What follows illustrates the way the staff at Uptown think and talk about the students for whom they are responsible. Consider Ben's words:

What I see is that a lot of kids are nowhere—they're not chatting, their mind is elsewhere, they're in another place. And I don't know if it's because there's such serious things that are bothering them. I don't know if it's just so much candy that they eat, or they didn't have breakfast. I don't know if it's because there's so much terror in the world recently. I don't know what it is.

This teacher believes that what could be labeled as student misbehavior is a consequence of their attention and energy being used up by their very real worries and difficulties that originate outside the classroom. He sees his job clearly—he needs to facilitate their learning of math and science. He is frustrated because the students are not fully ready to do this work. He is compassionate and concerned for their well-being. John continues the conversation:

John: The way, in math and science I thought that way. I'm starting to feel bad for the students that are really doing the work because there's obviously different levels in the class and um, I feel like students that demand a lot of attention demand a lot of attention because of their behaviors and then there's others who do the work who I could run on in a discussion with, but it's just, jelling all that.

Ben: I don't think it's, I don't think things are exactly the way we want them to be, and it's certainly not the way we planned for it to be. And, I don't think it's also a quick fix remedy type situation. For example, when we spoke, last week, or whenever it was, about SSR, about teaching reading, it keeps coming up to me that I should be teaching reading, I should be teaching a reading group because there are some kids who do read independently, you know, there's kids who need a reading group. I mean, I used to teach reading, right?, and there's kids that need that basically. I don't have a question about that. I know that that's the case. Whether SSR is the time to do it or whether we really need to look at, they need more attention from us, too, than we're able to give them on an individual basis. There's so many kids who I have to walk through everything, who can't go from square one to square two in an experiment. Who, in math, a lot of times are inaccurate simply because they don't get started, or if they get one thing down they do not know, they simply do not have the knowledge base to do the next thing which seems like they just never heard it. But it is hard, very hard. So it's like there's holes everywhere, and stuff is just leaking out all over the place. And the ones that are suffering are the, are either the ones who are attentive and trying to learn, or the ones who are, it's really around the ones who care and have a purpose, the ones who've got something to motivate them. But the ones also who are chatting and can't do this are suffering too, it just looks different. It looks different. They fake it best, they do other things to get past. Right. With their behavior that just doesn't pay attention.

Later in the conversation, Grace added:

> I have one kid who turns up for gym, for lunch, It's Jim, he's just working so hard, I'm just so proud of him. He doesn't have any time that he's not with me. And he loves me. I don't know, but . . . and he's really working hard with me, and he's a sweetheart, but it's really hard.

After Ben and John set up the conversation as an opportunity to share opinions and strategies, the rest of the staff took turns speaking about how they individually attended to their primary task of educating children who needed much more than math lessons. The collective work of keeping the staff aware of its identity as compassionate and effective educators was accomplished effectively during this staff meeting. Not incidentally, the entire conversation, ostensibly about student behavior in the classroom, was an episode of affirmation and building of a collective identity of compassionate, nurturing, and effective educators; using the social relations of community therapeutically for the benefit of the students; and drawing borders around themselves and the children whom they would teach and protect. In community, they would strive to keep the tragedies from outside from interfering with the education of their students.

LEARNING HOW TO LISTEN TO EACH OTHER

The remedial writing class, like Uptown, also functioned as a therapeutic community. To enroll in the class, students needed to test poorly on their writing placement tests and become labeled as in need of remediation. Their teachers were expected to facilitate their recovery from remediation into matriculation into the college. In addition to reading and writing practice, they chose to incorporate critically reflective conversations about the conditions of the student's lives, healing and therapeutic advice and inspiration, and the social relations of community into their classroom work. This implicit therapeutic function of the class brought vulnerability as its corollary.

As we saw earlier, much of the identity work done by the participants in the remedial writing class depended upon an inversion of the stigmatization placed upon the students (and by association, the teachers) by the college and the outside world. This was risky business for the students especially, for in order to invert their stigmatization, they had first to accept it and own it as valid and true. They were failed writers, linguistically deficient because they were linguistically different, physically and socially deficient because they were deaf (Robertson, 1995), politically inferior because they were poor, or women, or of ethnic minorities. Some were extremely fragile owing to the harrowing circumstances of their lives. One man, as a child, had seen his older sister shot and paralyzed, one man had been molested by his father, one woman was terrorized by her husband, several students were hospitalized for serious illnesses during the semester. The students were challenged by the teachers to consider these difficulties as struggles that would make them strong. They would become strong enough to become struggling writers, not failed writers. Perhaps they could become successful writers, matriculated college students, graduates, and ultimately successful adults. Enrique said:

> All right. It taught me a lot. It taught me too, the part that seemed her experience also seemed my experience, you know? I mean, struggling you know. I've struggled, I read and I have to do the papers. Now I

get sick, but I still gotta do the papers. Understand, that's a struggle, too! Understand? And I was in the hospital, and I was like, "Oh, God, where this lady's at?" But I still gotta read the book.

This was an enormous task, this mending of damaged identities, broken dreams, and battered bodies. They had to become successful writers, linguistically superior, powerful and strong.

Ernesto: Well, I mean, I never done it like this before. Looking at questions. I find it easier now. I'm just used to getting a book and reading. Then you tell me what the book is from ending to beginning. They never asked me about putting into my life the pages of the story.
Sharon: For you to relate, for you to think about.
Ernesto: Yeah, to relate [unintelligible] to put your lives in the book.
Sharon: What difference does that make for you, Ernesto?
Ernesto: Well now, when I read them, I think about my life too. And I try to put, I try to put it into the book, to see how it's similar or different from my own.
Sharon: And what does that do for the reading?
Ernesto: It makes you read a little closer, to understand more, to pick up more difficult things. Then, from there, I start to put my life into it too.
Sharon: Yeah. Right.
Ernesto: And I start thinking about my life a little more.
Sharon: Cause, as you say, you can see yourself in there. Or, you're curious. Am I in there? Or like, Enrique said, I mean, what different worlds, Helen Keller, you know, a White European woman born in this country, very wealthy, right. You know, and a young Dominican man in the Bronx. You see so many similarities in your life. And there can be, even though we be of seemingly different worlds. Out of the human condition, right, there are such similar drives and meanings and conflicts, right?

The students' resistance to writing was strong. Their shortcomings in this arena had been well documented through their previous failures with the WAT; lectures and in-class conversations during the semester referenced their past failures; and the end of the semester WAT was seen not only as the culminating event of the semester but as the concrete hurdle they would attempt to scale. They had no guarantee that their failure was at an end. Being a struggling writer was only marginally more appealing than being a failed writer. Engaging as a struggling writer necessitated some acknowledgment of personal responsibility for the previous failures and required continued attention to personal shortcomings. Adding the context of institutionalized impediments to success did not supplant personal accountability but rather made its failure more poignant.

Another significant impediment to writing for a number of students was that reading was also a difficult task. The deaf students had a particularly difficult time reading English, a common occurrence among the deaf population, whose average reading level is about that of a fourth grader. Although the deaf students had multiple challenges to reading and writing in English, they were not the only students who found the tasks daunting.

Individually, the students were not always sensitive to the struggles of their classmates. Although it was not difficult for the Urban U. students to talk about their common struggles in an unjust world, the scope of their empathy was tethered to an easy identification with their personal suffering. As a result, it was a much more arduous task to confront the injustices they themselves thoughtlessly perpetrated upon each other. Stretching their empathy, and consequent willingness to befriend each other, would only come with uncomfortable chagrin.

During the first half of the semester, the class negotiated regularly about how to communicate with each other. Most of these were brief, courteous, and pleasant encounters, but they were not always easy. Although there were affirmations of affiliation among the class members, it would be misleading to suggest that these glowing moments were the only expression of the negotiation of the boundaries and rules of the community. Sometimes there was war, as with Sharon:

> Stop. Stop. Stop! Please wait a minute, wait a minute. All right . . . as we said, in the community we have to, we have to agree upon certain things. But members in a community have a right, huh? So, I think what we need is Marcia wants to practice her signs. She needs the opportunity.

The above quote interrupted a rather chaotic scene caused by the adverse reaction of two of the deaf students to Marcia's hesitant signing. Sharon, impatient with their complaining, attempted to force a compromise that would afford Marcia the opportunity to practice her signing. She emphasized both the identity of the class as a community and the need to reach a compromise about communication modes that would not trample the rights of the individual participants. This negotiation made explicit a tension, and attendant vulnerability, between the common good and individual rights of the group (Bellah et al., 1985; Knight-Abowitz, 1997; Minow, 1990; Young, 1990). The border of fairness, the scope of their moral community, was at issue (Opotow, 1990).

Marcia, although deaf, had only recently learned to sign. Her signs were not fluent or clear, and her syntax was erratic. For that matter, her oral language was so soft as to be inaudible and, again, her use of syntax was not fluent. No matter whether she signed or spoke, the interpreter had difficulty in understanding her and in providing a smooth translation. The hard-of-hearing students could not understand her at all when she spoke, for they did not understand sign language.

Marcia had told us during the introductory class that she grew up hard of hearing in a household where Spanish was spoken, although she received her formal education in English. During the first ENFI conversation, Vanessa asked Marcia if learning sign language had been difficult for her. She replied:

> Vanessa, when i entered ntid (National Technical Institute for the Deaf) in rochestr i didnt know any sign language and it was very difficult to communicate with deaf people. so one day i asked my ex roommate to please teach me to sign language so i can communicate with other deaf people. it took me about two months to learn it but then i learn new sign, i am not 100%.

Much later, in April, she reiterated to us the history of her decision to designate herself as deaf rather than hard of hearing. By then, her decision to become fluent in ASL made sense to all the class members. But, at this time, only two friends in the class understood why it was so important for her to sign during this conversation.

The two deaf students who had objected to Marcia's signing were consistently assertive in ensuring that they could easily understand the conversations that dominated the class sessions. They, for example, always had a clear view of the interpreter. They were also insistent that the hearing students and the hard-of-hearing students accommodate them. But they were ignorant about the difficulties that even a member with acute hearing had in that classroom. The elevated subway line was a block away, across an open stretch of campus, and the trains whizzed by every few minutes, rattling the building and obscuring our words in roaring moments of noise. Even articulate speakers were hard to understand in that classroom.

However, the solution proposed, that there would be a simultaneous translation by the class interpreter (to English) and by the tutor (to sign) was received with strong disapproval by the two original protesters. They wouldn't know where to look, they would be confused, it wasn't fair. The proposed compromise ran counter to the current etiquette about accommodating the translation needs of the deaf participants in a class discussion. There was also an undercurrent of antipathy on the part of the deaf students for those who designated themselves hard of hearing. The hard of hearing, whose presence made the borders between the deaf and the hearing more clearly visible, were considered to be cravenly straddling a line between deaf and hearing cultures. And, at this time, Marcia had not strongly articulated her decision to designate herself as deaf (Padden & Humphries, 1988). Marcia gave up her attempts at signing that day, although she signed frequently during later classes.

It was important to reduce or eliminate the antipathy made visible during this event. Once it had become available to be explicitly examined, its demolition could be attempted. The building of the common identity of struggling writer was not necessarily dependent upon the eradication of perceived internal differences but rather upon their transformation into characteristics to honor. Working together cooperatively and courteously in order to communicate effectively was an honorable endeavor. The group's acceptance and tolerance of differences with significant political meaning would be a response to the vulnerability posed by the tension between the common good and individual rights. However, whether the response would support fracture or resilience would depend, in part, on agreement about what really was "common good." Although Sharon had consistently called the class a community, a community of writers, or a speech community, from the first day (Hymes, 1972a, 1972b), the acceptance of this identity as a common good was not a given. Skepticism about the triumphantly transformative power of identity was never demolished, and resistance to both identity and practice was strong. Although the students grew in their willingness to support each other, the semester was too short a time to learn if this willingness to be supportive could be trusted. The development of trust in the power of empathic support would need to be proven as a reliable element in the practice of a community of writers. Only working extensively on their writing together could prove it.

RECOGNITION

Even in a school where difference and diversity must be sanitized or ignored, there needs to be some way of recognizing or creating tolerable differentiation among the students. One way to do this is to recognize participation in events that evoke an overall sense of community identity. Honoring the achievements of teachers or students, for example, makes it clear to all what practices or attitudes are valued. Similarly, public admonishment or shunning makes it clear what practices or attitudes are not valued by the group. Such rites are important markers of group norms and values, and thus useful tools in the teaching and learning of how to be a competent member of the group. In addition, they are powerfully valenced within community. They carry the power to evoke an emotional response, to evoke, for example, recognizable feelings of connection and disconnection among the participants.

Rites of passage, enhancement, degradation, integration, conflict reduction, and renewal are employed in schools for various purposes. Among the diverse uses of these public events is their utility in marking the enrichment or danger of diversity and difference to the group (Cohen, 1985; McDermott, 1994). Rites of passage, enhancement, and degradation focus attention on individuals in the service of sustaining community or an idealized version of community in the school.

At Uptown and St. Margaret's Academy Elementary School, such events occurred regularly. For example, at Uptown there was a daily break from 10:10 A.M. until 10:20 A.M., a time for students and teachers to relax, visit the bathrooms, and so on. This break time was a treasured opportunity for the students to congregate in two places: the gym and the office. Both places have been described as the "heart" of the school, for here routine but cherished community activities took place. More than half of the students chatted, made plans, listened to music, danced, played a fast game of basketball, and otherwise connected socially in the gym during this time. Dozens of the other students rushed to the office to cajole food, a Band-Aid, or a conversation from the school secretary, director, and any other adult who might be in the room. Teachers also found their way to the office at this time, for similar reasons. Break time was time to attend to valued social relations of community at Uptown.

St. Margaret's similarly had a daily time to make some social relations of community visible—its morning meeting, when prayers and announcements were interspersed with more entertaining events, such as brief student presentations. Staff meetings at both St. Margaret's Elementary and High Schools marked community as they began with formal ceremonies that included prayer and opportunities for reflection. Prayers often marked the beginning and end of classes and, in the elementary school, grace was said before dismissal for lunch. The prayers praised, petitioned, or thanked God—a palpable reminder of the spiritual family that has God as its parent. The prayers were recited aloud and in unison, marked by a few permissible practices such as clasped or upraised hands, bowed heads, and the absence or significant diminishment of conversation. Interruptions were not acceptable. The daily prayers were also included in every ceremony, celebration, or meeting that formally marked the school as in community, such as the music and art exhibition, a fundraising meeting for parents, field day, and recognition night. There were many times when students or teachers asked for prayers for a parent's or a sibling's health, or for comfort during bereavement. These prayers were offered as an expression of care and connection, as a way to share joy and sorrow.

Both Uptown and St. Margaret's also had other occasions during which they celebrated a sense of community. Uptown had its Festival of Lights, an early winter celebration for the staff, students, and their families, an annual play written and performed by students, and, most important, weekly Friday afternoon excursions for the entire school. In the winter months, these often were trips to a nearby public ice-skating rink (Foresta, 1996).

Mass was celebrated for the St. Margaret's Academy Elementary School community the first Thursday of each month. This monthly Mass was a celebration of the spiritual community of which the members of the school were part. One class took responsibility for the readings, offerings, and music for each Mass. The school's chaplain officiated at the Mass, and many of the retired Sisters who lived in the convent on the school grounds attended. At every Mass I attended, the homily included references to our spiritual family.

Another way of celebrating the norms of community in a community of learners is to make academic achievement a public occasion of celebration. At St. Margaret's Academy Elementary School, as at Uptown School, recognition for success was given to students for both academic and nonacademic achievements, but in contrast to Uptown, St. Margaret's placed more emphasis on academic achievement than on other laudable student practices. Placement on the school honor roll was the reward for high report-card grades at St. Margaret's and was determined by a preset formula. The design and control of the recognition were in the hands of the whole staff at Uptown and were re-considered on a monthly basis. Recognition was given to students who needed it at Uptown at least as often as to those who earned it in more traditional ways. Categories of honor, such as students of the month, were created at Uptown whenever deemed appropriate. In both schools, the recognition and awards created, acknowledged, and celebrated acceptable manifestations of internal difference and diversity in the service of supporting a sense of community and group identity.

For example, at St. Margaret's Academy there was an end-of-year recognition ceremony for the graduates. Student participation and accomplishment in nonacademic areas, such as basketball and yearbook preparation, were acknowledged. In addition, the ceremonies included "recognition" (words of thanks and praise) of parents and teachers. The act of recognition was an important reinforcer of the school-wide sense of community. It celebrated the ideals and values of the group by honoring those who exemplified them. Performed for staff and parents by those about to leave this community, it was a testament to the loving bonds that wrapped them tightly together as well as an event to be recalled later in fond reminiscence. My field notes state that on Recognition Night,

> The school gym was filled with parents and family members of the graduating class, as well as with the entire school staff and some of the Sisters of the Congregation who lived in the convent on the grounds. After the eighth graders entered and were seated facing the audience, the principal of the school asked the families to stand and extend their

hands toward their daughters in blessing, as she prayed aloud. Three students read aloud "memories" that recognized the significant moments of their school experiences. The eighth grade teacher took her turn to "recognize some of the achievements of the class of 1994." She cited fundraising, school spirit, class helpers, Girl Scouts and their leader, Confirmations, yearbook work, the selection of one of the students as a cellist in the county student orchestra. She named students in each category. They stood as their names were called. When the teacher finished, a long round of applause ensued. A parent who taught three of the girls Russian language and culture on Saturdays "recognized" their achievements. The principal recognized achievers in art and music. The gym teacher announced the Most Valuable Player award for the basketball team was earned by a 7th grader. It would be given to her during the last morning meeting, when the rest of the students received their recognition and achievement awards.

Academic awards were announced for the final trimester. Seven of the twenty-four students were awarded second honors for maintaining averages between 90 and 94%. Nine students were awarded first honors, for maintaining an average between 95 and 99%. Again, each student stood and was applauded when her name was called.

After the students had been recognized, they in turn thanked and praised their teachers and parents. Each teacher was individually recognized by a student who spoke briefly of how that teacher was special. After recognizing a teacher, the girl went to her or him, and bestowed a kiss and a small wrapped gift (a china picture frame). Applause followed each recognition.

Then the tears began to flow in the audience as the students recognized their parents for their loving support. Each student gave a rose to her parents as a symbol of love and recognition.

Recognition Night was an event eagerly anticipated and carefully planned for by the eighth-grade students and their teacher. But the inclusion of the formal recognition with its accompanying words of praise and thanks was not always smoothly accomplished. For example, in June of 1993, some of the students did not want to "recognize" several teachers. Although some students told me they felt embarrassment at their ungracious attitude, their antipathy to carrying out the assignment was clear. Yet they could not refuse to participate. Such refusal was not tolerated by their teacher. Even though this group of eighth graders did not share a strong sense of being in community with each other or with the whole school, they would have to act as if they did. This was a necessary part of appropriately being eighth graders at St. Margaret's Academy. The acting out of a traditional event for others within community could not be avoided without chipping away at the security of the collective school identity of loving family. The students had no option but to participate in this important ritual of recognition.

Doing one's best was always appropriate, but appropriate competition required that there be no losers. A distinction was made between giving recognition and giving awards. Everyone was entitled to recognition for his or her appropriate work and achievements. Competition for the relatively scarce academic and athletic honors was both encouraged and discouraged. Because academic honors and awards were given at report-card times and at the end-of-the-year ceremonies, their pursuit was implicitly encouraged. But some of the students and their families, according to staff members, unfortunately overemphasized the value of the acquisition of such awards and honors. This was inappropriate and to be discouraged. Doing well, and only coincidentally garnering "recognition" for one's achievements, was appropriate. An overemphasis on competition for honors or awards was understood to potentially interfere with the desired attitudes toward others that contributed to a sense of loving connection at St. Margaret's. It was important to refrain from turning student achievement into factionalizing competition for the rewards of achievement.

I interviewed the gym teacher at St. Margaret's Academy Elementary School, who explained to me how he undermined the potential of competitiveness to create tension among the students. He told me: "I always try to make it as a tie. Then nobody wins, but they all won. Because, (1) they had a good time and (2) they all tried their best out there. So nobody wins and nobody's feelings are hurt." Competition here had little to do with winning or losing. Rather, it meant doing one's best, and enjoying doing one's best. The gym teacher called this sportsmanship.

SINGING THE BLUES

The celebration of community may be marked by planned moments of recognition, as often happened at Uptown and St. Margaret's, but also arises spontaneously, at unexpected moments. Sadly, too, the planned moments of community celebration, the longed-for triumphant rites of passage, can mark the fracturing of community instead of celebrating its resilience. The struggling writers of the Urban U. remedial writing class lived through such contrasting occasions.

There were some sweet episodes of uncluttered and clear communion among the students and teachers. One moment occurred 2 days after a devastating fire had swept through a Bronx social club, leaving many people dead. Serious, intense conversation about oppressive social conditions and inequities took up much of the class time, and the mood of the class, hearing and deaf, matched the dreary day. Forty-five minutes was devoted to this discussion, and references to the discussion crept into the analysis of writing that followed. Sharon, the instructor, spoke forcefully and at length about the craft of writing, emphasizing the importance of the process of composition. Sharon compared the artistic component of writing with that of music, specifically the arrangement of the appropriate elements in a harmonious composition.

After half an hour of writing analysis, the atmosphere began to lighten. The talk became more abstract as the exploration of writing as an art continued. Sharon explained the difference between modeling one's work on that of another artist and merely copying that work. She turned to Charles, a young, shy, gentle African American musician and singer wrapped in a huge black leather trench coat, and asked him to tell who his musical models were. Denise wanted to know what type of music they sang. The discussion took a delightful turn as Sharon expanded the emerging metaphor of composition to include an impromptu demonstration.

"How do deaf people know about types of music?" Sharon challenged the hearing students. "They can't hear it!" She asked Charles if he could describe rhythm and blues to the deaf students.

> Rhythm, what I mean by rhythm and blues, rhythm is the beat of the music. Or when you snap your fingers you get a beat. Or when you stamp your feet, you have a beat. Blues is a feeling that you have, uh, at a particular time of day you just lost your girlfriend, you and your girlfriend just broke up, so you feel down. So they would call that a case of the blues. . . . How it happens is that with the blues you have a feeling of being sad, so you pick a type of music that would fit that type of moment in that musician.

Charles agreed to sing the blues for us. He snapped his fingers, tapped his foot, and closed his eyes. His face was serious. We all intently watched his face as we listened. The interpreter was sitting two seats away from Charles, so the deaf students could, fortuitously, read both her signs and Charles's face. This juxtaposition of singer and interpreter was instrumental in ensuring comprehension of the essential message of Charles's song: the rhythm and the melancholy. This short rendition led Charles to explain further:

> He's trying to create an atmosphere. He also trying to create a feeling for somebody else, so if they were feeling that same way, they could understand what that person was going through.

Charles was doing the same thing—creating an atmosphere, sharing a feeling that he demonstrated in his music. The discussion continued, with both deaf and hearing participants questioning and commenting freely. As students questioned Charles about the blues, he spoke of variations within the genre. He mentioned happy blues, and Sharon beamed and nodded as she stood at her desk. Not understanding the concept of happy blues, I asked for elucidation. Sharon responded with an amusing example of a woman who had been wronged by her man, and then shot him!

Charles was requested to sing again, this time a happy blues. He sang "Flat Foot Floogie," and it was terrific! His voice and gestures were eloquent; there were many smiles, swaying bodies, and tapping toes among the other members of the class.

A fledgling sense of community grew stronger that afternoon, making it possible for a shy young man to dare to sing for a dozen other people, and to convey, by his affect, just what the blues could mean. Spontaneous applause followed his performance. Enrique, a hearing Latino man, led the applause, waving his arms silently above his head in the ASL manner. Many of the hearing participants followed suit, blurring the languages as the students expressed their growing sense of affiliation with each other. Over the span of the semester, there were other examples of such use of simple ASL by the hearing students, but none so moving. Gumperz (1972) discusses the significance of such code switching for bi-dialectical and bilingual members of a community. The switch from one language to another is not random but is often used to indicate deep emotion or affiliation. Within this particular context, the use of ASL by the hearing students served to reinforce the intimacy and sense of connection that had been established in the preceding hours, and in the preceding weeks. It was used as a marker of group membership, as a move by the students to deepen their sense of connectedness to each other. The hand-clapping applause by the deaf students served the same purpose. Because Charles shared his emotions with them, they expressed their appreciation to him in his own language, as an acknowledgment of their communality.

The analysis of writing as an art akin to music was a delightfully enriching moment during the class. The somber and angry group who began the class preoccupied with the devastating fire were relaxed and smiling as they discussed the comparison of musical and written composition. The discussion of the blues seemed to be an almost accidental enhancement of the theme but was actually skillfully engineered by Sharon, who challenged Charles to describe what he knew. Her purpose was to make a connection with the description used in good writing, in order to encourage further analysis by the students. She was able to bring closure to the musical aside by tying it in again with the creation of an atmosphere, of a feeling, in good writing.

Because Charles's explanation was contextualized in a situation where he could gesture, where he could quickly assess and adjust his comprehensibility, the communication was quite competent (Hymes, 1972a, 1972b; Long & Porter, 1985). He was questioned by Denise and Mai, two of the deaf women, for example, which encouraged him to continue his explanation and performance. If Charles had been requested to write his demonstration of the meaning of the blues, for example, he may not have been so eloquent. He would have needed to fit his emotion into the rigorously correct syntax expected by the WAT assessors.

The context provided an almost irresistible opportunity to use linguistic obstacles such as the inability to develop toward what Hymes (1972a) calls a speech community: "[a] community sharing rules for the conduct and interpretation of speech, and rules for the interpretation of at least one linguistic variety" (p. 54). However close the group had drawn to becoming a speech community, and however sweet was their emerging sense of community, a significant omission would still impact on their coalescence as a community of writers. They still were not writing as their central practice.

The students and teachers earnestly went about the work of using community therapeutically as the semester progressed. Oral, signed, and written conversations were not the only avenues through which they worked. A growing sense of affiliation was also expressed physically. All class participants usually sat together in an inward-facing circle at every class, but this pattern broke when the students were requested to regroup for small-group discussion late in April (see Figure 4.2).

As the hour progressed, the students managed to arrange themselves in a series of linked groups, diverse as to language used and as to race, gender, and age, whose boundaries were less and less clear as the afternoon wore on. Nelson, the isolate, remained somewhat disconnected from the group, indicating his own conflicted sense of identity and group membership.

By the end of the session, all but one of the students were closely huddled together, connected, presenting what might be interpreted as their best defense against the onerous task they had yet to face, the WAT. This defense was to physically and emotionally align themselves as a mutually dependent, interconnected community of real writers (Atwell, 1987).

They had spent close to 4 months reaching this instance of reduced dependency on the teacher and increased reliance upon each other. The writers supported each other's efforts by reading and offering suggestions and comments; they offered their care and concern, and emphasized their interconnected lives by their tight alignment. For an hour the class acted as if they were real writers, and the flickering of resilient community was apparent. But was it too late? How much activity as real writers would be needed to transform their vulnerability into resilience?

Figure 4.2. Writing conference configurations

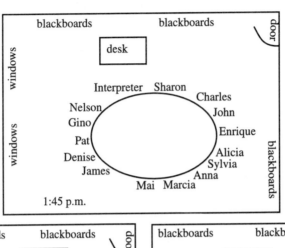

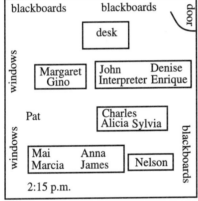

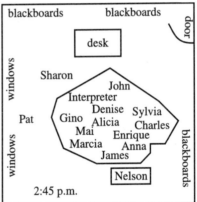

The students' concentration on the reading/writing task assigned may have been prompted by the knowledge that the first WAT was scheduled for 1 week later and that they needed to work seriously on their writing. As I watched them huddle together, I projected that they were actually quite apprehensive about taking the exam, which they had all failed before. The evolution of a caring community was one thing, perhaps, and the test was another entirely. They knew that they would be assessed by the college solely on their solitary performances on the test, and they seemed to seek reassurance that their writing abilities would measure up. The test, despite the urgent exhortations of the teachers and their own assertions on March 20, mattered to them.

When I entered the classroom on the afternoon of the Writing Assessment Test, the circle of desks had disappeared (see Figure 4.3). The students had taken seats far from each other. One student, Mai, moved her desk to an isolated corner of the room and faced a lonely corner. Denise turned her desk completely around, so that she was facing the back wall, totally isolating herself from the class and from the interpreter. During the exam, several students bolted from the room, and some did not return for quite some time. After the test was over, I asked Charles why he had left. He replied that he couldn't stand the tension.

Had they maintained their usual circle, their conferences, their sense of connectedness, might they have been able to face the test as a community of real writers and not as the collection of not-yet-writers or failed writers that the WAT had always designated them? But, as mentioned before, the WAT was not constructed or used to measure writing as a collaborative activity but only as a solitary effort.

The students and teachers, in their statements during the semester, had ostensibly demolished the power of the WAT, but their behavior during the WAT indicated otherwise. They isolated themselves, were visibly nervous, some physically ill, all tense and quiet. Now they were simply individuals in the same room, about to undergo the same ordeal. They took the test the way they had always taken the test, alone.

Figure 4.3. Seating during the writing assessment test

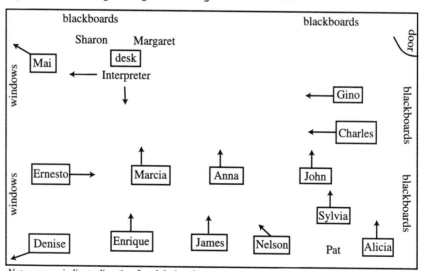

Note: arrows indicate direction faced during the test.

Their understanding of the test's implications for the meaning of writing was clear. Perhaps they were indeed a community of writers, but the test could not measure the collaborative construction of meaning implied by the notion of community. So they could not take the test in community. The entwined messages were clear: You are a community of writers; and you are failed writers (Blot, personal communication, 1991). The WAT cannot measure your worth as individuals, as a community, as writers; but you must take it anyway. Solidarity and mutual empowerment had been envisioned by the teachers as more potentially beneficial to the students than repetitive practice for the written exam could ever be. But the benefits were not to be measured during that semester. Although several of the students improved their academic writing, and many expressed the deepest gratitude to the teachers for structuring the course as they did, only two students, both hearing, passed the exam.

CHAPTER 5

Vulnerability, Fragility, and Resilience in Community

In Chapter 1, I stated that certain conditions must exist if community is to arise and flourish. Each group studied was able to create, even if only briefly, the four conditions (group identity, accounting for internal diversity, ways to learn how to become competent, and celebrations) that accompany the rise of practices and feelings about these practices that are recognized as community. However, it is apparent from the trajectory of the remedial writing class that unless the conditions are held long enough and strongly enough, community is not likely to flourish. In addition, although successful maintenance of these conditions can arise in the normal give and take of the everyday practices of group members, if the idea of community is imposed upon a group rather than generated from within, it may not take hold within the group's practices.

Three of the groups were successful in building resilient community through their practices. It is significant that these three groups were less concerned with the notion of community than with the education of their students. All three schools were able to maintain the necessary conditions for establishing community as they went about the business of educating their students. The staffs in all three schools, but especially in Uptown and in St. Margaret's Academy High School, believed that they were in professional community. Thus the group that successfully builds community may consider the social relations of community as incidental, although important to its other practices. In fact, the one group studied here in which the notion of community was more prominent than the notion of practice failed to build resilient community.

The remedial writing class could not maintain two of the necessary conditions for the building of community. Their sense of community identity was never securely established, and they did not learn how to master what ought to have been the central practice of their community. They had moments of communion, which, as explained earlier, are not reliant upon the existence of community. These moments of communion, however, fell short of building resilience in community. The few rituals and ceremonies available to the group made the fatal flaws more apparent. The one instance of group conferencing about writing, potentially a source of celebrating their ostensible central practice, was too rare and too late. It became a foreshadow of the disappointment to come.

There is a relationship between the nature of community at each site and the work to which it was put. Two of the groups studied were self-consciously engaged in attempts at transformation. Two were self-consciously engaged in maintaining tradition. The nature of community, its form and function, was unique at each site in part because of the nature of the work it does at each.

This relationship drew on the strong normative powers of community in both the Catholic schools. The normative work is believed to create a close family within the elementary school and competent ninth graders in the high school. The relations tentatively drew on the identity-transformative powers of the process of communal support to maintain a struggle against a hostile institution in the remedial writing class. The longed-for transformative power of community alone, however, was not strong enough to overcome the power of the university's gatekeeping exam. At Uptown School, community was envisioned as the path through the opening doorway of school transformation. This dream of community as rescue from the pervasive poor consequences of urban schooling propelled much collaborative and reflective inquiry at Uptown School.

As the words, practices, and beliefs of the participants at the four school sites demonstrate, the construction of identity was accomplished differently at each location, reflecting the differing nature of community at each. The membership was necessarily different in each group because of the specific nature of the educational institution, but only in the remedial writing class was this limiting of potential membership considered to be ominously significant by insiders. Only in Uptown School did the internal differences and diversity of its members have the capacity to powerfully influence any aspect of group identity. For all three other groups, internal diversity and difference were made significant or insignificant in order to align with and support well-established group identity. The difference in the primacy of group identity held implications for the ways in which community could demonstrate its resilience in the schools. Uptown's practices of resilience demonstrated adaptation rather than intractability, but in the two private schools, resilience was demonstrable in the inviolability of their group identities. The members of the writing class, in contrast, had neither an acceptable, well-established group identity nor a satisfactory resolution of how to deal with their internal differences. See Table 5.1.

In order to support the notion of an all-inclusive spiritual community, St. Margaret's Academy Elementary School arranged its practices to support beliefs about essential spiritual and embodied equality, spiritual commonality, and spiritual family. Further internal distinctions, such as the notion of tolerance of diversity, supported the group's belief about their inclusiveness but required diminishing or ignoring certain kinds of differences, such as their existing economic and gendered exclusionary practices. They used conformity and a "zone

Table 5.1 Elements of group identity

	St. Margaret's Academy Elementary School	St. Margaret's Academy High School	Uptown School	Remedial Writing Class
Boundary	public schools with regard to values and the organization of teaching and learning, internally perceived as open to all within spiritual family	academic rigor in comparison with other high schools	all other schools	the university, successful writers
Border	not perceived as important by insiders, perceived as economic and gender-limited by outsiders	myth of familial commonality imposed from inside, limited by economics, gender, and religious affiliation	professional identity	the WAT
Group identity	spiritual family, real family	intergenerational family	professional community, caring family	struggling writers who honor their differences and stigmatized failed writers; marginalized, incompetent writers
Type	functional community: spiritual lifetime spiritual membership transcends school setting	functional community: faith intergenerational membership transcends school setting	values community and community of practice: professional/limited tenure of membership only relevant within school setting	Community of practice: writers 15-week tenure of membership only relevant within the class
Values and beliefs	common core of values and beliefs affirmed by all members values and beliefs are cohesive	common core of values and beliefs affirmed by all members values and beliefs are cohesive	open/multiple sets of beliefs and values assembled by members values and beliefs may be cohesive, compete and/or conflict	unstable core of values and beliefs assembled by members values and beliefs compete

of silence" to ensure practices that supported beliefs about inclusiveness and tolerance. Like the elementary school, the high school considered itself to be a family. Relying on the power of tradition and rigid normative practices, group members demanded appropriate attitude at the expense of diversity.

Uptown School, on the other hand, defined its group identity differently. Shared beliefs about an all inclusive spiritual family could not be central to their group and did not influence the group to find ways to support that identity. Rather, the group identity of professional community and values community around progressive education led to different ways of marking the participants' distinctiveness from each other. Staff decision-making was one such practice that built group identity. The management of consensus, dissent, and leadership was arranged to accommodate beliefs about how professional community devotes attention "to the kids" without sacrificing individual choice. The sense of professionalism, however, that supported professional practice came not from long-standing tradition but from the daily interactions the staff had with each other and with the students. Table 5.2 captures elements of internal diversity that were prominent at each site.

Table 5.2 Management of internal difference and diversity

St. Margaret's Academy Elementary School	*St. Margaret's Academy High School*	*Uptown School*	*Remedial Writing Class*
spiritual commonality	commonality and tradition	attention to individual students	common stigma
myth of family	myth of family	staff as decision-makers	stigma into honor
diversity tolerated if insignificant	diversity treated as nonexistent	differences and diversity stressed	diversity and differences explored
conformity and uniformity	difference not tolerated	individuality	neutralized difference
appropriate behavior demanded	proper attitude demanded by staff and students	curricular innovations	critical analysis of common struggles
"zone of silence" maintained		power of subgroups is restricted	
		consensus and democracy	

Table 5.3 highlights the management of consensus and dissent by each group.

Learning how to be in community was among the most important work done in all four sites. The success of learning the norms of community, however, varied from site to site. The two Catholic schools were most successful in indoctrinating their newcomers and training their members to internalize community norms. These schools' longevity contributed to this success, of course. Well-established norms are powerful, and mature community members have had much experience in affirming and sustaining them.

However, longevity alone does not fuel normative forces. This rigorous normative thrust was a response, in St. Margaret's Academy Elementary and High Schools, to their understanding of deviance as a threat to community. Any deviance from the norms of behavior and attitude demanded in the high school, for example, carried the possibility of revelation of the mythic elements of their "family." In addition, their distaste for deviance revealed the shaky foundations of their tolerance for difference and diversity. Thus rendering difference and diversity insignificant served to lessen the potential fracturing of community that could result.

In a newer school like Uptown, there had been only a handful of years to develop and affirm norms. Also, because of the evolving coherence of community at Uptown, norms were difficult to establish with clarity or with any

Table 5.3 Management of dissent and consensus

St. Margaret's Academy Elementary School	St. Margaret's Academy High School	Uptown School	Remedial Writing Class
divergent opinions are kept silent	divergent opinions are kept silent	divergent opinions become consensus	divergent opinions are discussed
		reflective conversations dominate	critical conversations dominate
"zone of silence" operates	appropriate attitude is enforced		teacher controls voice
authoritative decisions	authoritative decisions	democracy and consensus	mediated by teacher
acceptance of authority	acceptance of authority	negotiated authority	acceptance of teacher authority

guarantee of permanence. In fact, their particular emphasis on attending to individuals and celebrating diversity may have precluded the establishment of intransigent norms. The students and the staff cooperated with great faith in their capacity to discover how best to act. Deviance was not a threat at Uptown, where conformity and docility were not highly valued. Table 5.4 shows some of the important elements that group members attended to when learning how to be in community and when celebrating community.

THE VULNERABILITY OF COMMUNITY

There is a vulnerability inherent in the risk of choosing to be in community. Some of the groups in this study were in this vulnerable free-fall of community building. Their sense of themselves as being in community was fragile and uncertain. The remedial writing class worked earnestly to feel a sense of community, for community was promised to help them pass the WAT. Uptown teachers grew stronger in their sense of community as they carried out their roles, but as we saw, a sense of community was sometimes a fleeting phenomenon among Uptown students. Other groups, such as the students in the Catholic elementary school, were confident and secure in their belief that they were in community.

There were differences among groups at each site in their beliefs about whether they were in community or not. For example, the new ninth graders at St. Margaret's Academy High School were not at all confident about being in community and worked diligently to become secure. The school staff, on the other hand, knew with certainty that they were in community and confidently carried out their practices and beliefs. Similarly, the staff at St. Margaret's Academy Elementary School undertook in good faith to teach their students how to be good and appropriate members of their community.

Recent research (Bryk et al., 1993; Sergiovanni, 1994) indicates that the existence of community in schools may be one of the most essential components of successful schools. But sustaining community in school is challenged and sometimes threatened by its inherent vulnerabilities. I believe the task is less to purge the community of such vulnerabilities than to understand and utilize them to build resilient community.

One such vulnerability was made visible by the presence of subgroups within the larger group. At Uptown and St. Margaret's Academy Elementary School, groups such as the Boy Talk and Girl Talk classes or the discontented eighth graders opened areas of community vulnerability. The sophomores with attitude at St. Margaret's High School sat uncomfortably in the cafeteria, and the deaf and hard-of-hearing students in the remedial writing class were separated by an ideological tension, marking the cohesiveness of group identity as

Table 5.4 Elements of learning how to be in community and celebrating community

	St. Margaret's Academy Elementary School	St. Margaret's Academy High School	Uptown School	Remedial Writing Class
Identity	clearly defined, competence grows	clearly defined, little flexibility is tolerated	professional identity well developed	conflicted, marginal status in university
Idealized versions of identity	essential to maintain, not subject to critique	essential to maintain, not subject to critique	in development, subject to critique and revision	conflicted
Myths	prevalent, not subject to deconstruction	prevalent, not subject to deconstruction	critiqued and debunked if not substantiated	not seen as reality but as wish fulfillment
Diversity and difference	only insignificant difference is tolerable	conformity is necessary to continue traditions	diversity and difference very important	antipathy among subgroups, ignorance of others' needs
Dissent	irrelevant	hierarchical decisions	taken seriously	not tolerated
Consensus	irrelevant	assumed to be implicit	highly valued	irrelevant

Special interests	ignored	vigorously eradicated	valued but controlled	dismissed as irrelevant
Conflicting ideals	irrelevant	irrelevant	respected	irrelevant
Norms	clear, strictly enforced	clear, strictly enforced	not consolidated, in flux	not established
Resistance to normative practices	weak	weak	sincere and open	insignificant
Democracy	insignificant	insignificant	significant	irrelevant
Conformity	valued, significant	significant	not valued, avoided	insignificant
Academic pursuits	explicit instruction, no individualized curricula	tracked classes, explicit instruction	individualized, learning is facilitated	writing not practiced enough
Celebration	regular and frequent, scheduled	regularly scheduled	regular and frequent, scheduled and impromptu	neither regular nor frequent, spontaneous

vulnerable to discordance. Did attending to those and other vulnerabilities make community more resilient or more fragile? The answer to the question is not simple. For example, resilience and fragility clearly existed in uncertain balance at Uptown School and in the remedial writing class. Many events at either place revealed or engendered resilience and fragility simultaneously. However, any hint of fragility resulting from vulnerabilities was quite threatening in the private schools, with the result that vigorous attempts to eradicate vulnerabilities were made before they could fragment the group. If vulnerabilities could not be reduced, they were ignored with little negative impact felt by the dominant group insiders. Those who felt the impact of ignored vulnerabilities either learned ways to accommodate their burden or suffered the sting of normative sanctions.

The relations between vulnerability, fragility, and resilience may be such that moments and spaces of vulnerability and even fragility are necessary components of the fostering of resilient community. Fissures and fractures are not always the products of fragility and vulnerability. Strength and resilience can also result. Practices that demonstrate strength and resilience may need occasions of vulnerability and the threat of fragility to spur their emergence. Some internal control over these moments and spaces might be desirable to maintain, similar to those controls in evidence at St. Margaret's Academy Elementary and High Schools. However, it isn't always possible to manage these moments or spaces in the interest of providing opportunities to exercise community resilience. Too stringent control of potential fragile moments or spaces may paradoxically erode the habits of resilience. Then, even the least vulnerability may result in grievous fissures and fractures to community. Consider the alarm caused by the eighth-grade food fight at St. Margaret's Academy Elementary School, for example. Without practices in place to openly acknowledge and deal with the tensions of difference and diversity among the students, any exposition of these was seen as risking serious damage to the group sense of identity and to its continued harmonious, tolerant existence.

We have seen that the carrying out of certain events is not without consequences for the process of community. The management of consensus and leadership during staff decision-making at Uptown, for example, manifestly making it possible for the staff to get on with its work, influenced how people felt about themselves in relation to the others with whom they worked. When consensus was a match among everyone's opinions, for example, the staff celebrated their sense of being in community together. However, if consensus or leadership was achieved at the expense of silenced staff members, they felt betrayed and resentful. They not only felt that they were out of community but also then tended to arrange additional practices that widened the rift they felt. When the group sense of being in community was threatened by conversation or stated opinions, vigilant protection of their group identity was employed. Sometimes this type of interaction healed actual or potential rifts, but the risk that such protective gestures would reinforce feelings of being out of community was always present.

If subgroups within the school engaged in talk or practices that brought attention to issues that could factionalize the larger group, compensatory practices were arranged. We were able to see this vividly in Uptown's disposition of the future of the Girl Talk and Boy Talk classes.

From an outside perspective, actions taken by a group may seem to contain unfortunate consequences for some of the participants. The sacrifice of one's racial or ethnic identity, for example, or the adoption of proper "attitude" are coerced responses to inflexible demands for the conformity and uniformity that marked membership in the St. Margaret's Academy High School family. From the inside perspective, however, these practices are in the interest of the community as a whole and are thus desirable and valued. The absolute certainty with which the staff could inculcate certain behaviors in the students was proudly seen as one of the central strengths of the school.

Similarly, the enforcement of appropriate attitudes, language, beliefs, and practices in each of the Catholic schools is practiced with the intention of helping the students become competent community members. The resulting uniformity makes it possible to be a family in the elementary school. The sacrifice of the possibility of student discovery of new knowledge, for example, is not noticed, or is considered a reasonable accommodation.

The vulnerability of the remedial writing students could not be lessened despite every effort. In the face of an institution in which the class was a stigmatized inclusion, student victory over the stigmatizing WAT was almost impossible. The reality of the power of the university to continue to use the WAT to judge them deficient overshadowed any progress they could have made together as a community of writers.

The gap between how group members idealized their community and the actual practices in which they engaged was a site of vulnerability for community at all places. At St. Margaret's Academy Elementary School the greatest threat to the resilience of community occurred if the myth of family could not be maintained. Tolerance for diversity was not unconditional but was practiced if the diversity was insignificant.

At St. Margaret's Academy High School, diversity was intolerable, and so the St. Margaret's students learned how to normalize themselves through intensive moral regulation, normative practices that produce individuals who adhere to implicit and explicit rules of conduct and conscience as if these were naturally self-generated and monitored (Calderwood, 1998b; Rousmaniere, Dehli, & de Coninck-Smith, 1997).

Tables 5.5 and 5.6 highlight some of the strengths and fragilities of community for each group. It is significant that the two strengths listed for the remedial writing class were but possibilities, whereas the fragilities were real and numerous.

Table 5.5 Strengths of community at each site

St. Margaret's Academy Elementary School	St. Margaret's Academy High School	Uptown School	Remedial Writing Class
spiritual community is inclusive and enduring	inter-generational family is enduring	staff is a professional community	transformation of stigma into honor could have promoted valued identities
trusting relations are sustained	clear guidelines for appropriate behavior are accepted	trusting relations are sustained	critical analysis of situated lives could have been a transformative act
clear guidelines for academic and social behaviors create a sense of orderliness	clear expectations support students' academic achievement and staff professional identity	students' social needs are addressed and often met	
the myth of family is sustained	the myth of family is sustained	consideration of and attempted eradication of internal inequities	
notion of tolerance remains salient	tradition continues	group adapts to challenges	
identity is not conflicted	identity is not conflicted	identity and practice change in response to new needs	
professional practice effective	professional practice effective	professional practice effective	

Table 5.6 Fragility of community at each site

St. Margaret's Academy Elementary School	St. Margaret's Academy High School	Uptown School	Remedial Writing Class
myth of family cannot eliminate pervasive differences	myth of family requires sacrifice of personal identity	forced consensus can result in sabotage, resentment, abdication of decision-making responsibilities	transformation of stigma did not eliminate gatekeeper power
significant differences are ignored, existing tensions are not addressed	any deviation from appropriate "attitude" causes discord	pockets of inclusion and communion can factionalize the group	transformation of stigma did not increase writing skill
		attending to individual student needs sometimes creates secrecy and erosion of trust	important differences continued to factionalize students
			realistic assessment of situated lives resulted in resignation for some students
			professional practice was not effective

TRANSFORMING VULNERABILITY INTO RESILIENCE

What was the secret to the successful maintenance of resilient community at St. Margaret's Academy Elementary School? Perhaps the most important factor was its long history as a successful educational institution (Blot & Calderwood, 1995). There was a clarity of purpose in the practices of the staff: They would attend to the whole child. The inculcation of goodness and appropriateness supported the ways in which diversity was made tolerable, as did the organization of the teaching and learning of academic matters. The resulting harmony and trusting relations supported a strong sense of being in community as well as practices that affirmed their long-standing resilient community. Vulnerabilities were managed through reduction or by ignoring them. The group members, although highly valuing their notions of community and their sense of being in community, paid much less attention to the idea of community than to their central practices of teaching and learning academic subjects, and inculcating goodness and appropriateness. (See figure 5.1)

How were the students and staff at St. Margaret's Academy High School able to build resilient community? They, too, had entered into long-standing resilient community. They successfully used rigorous application of normative practices to maintain this tradition intact. As at St. Margaret's Academy Elementary School, the students and faculty of the high school poured most of their efforts into academic pursuits and into the management of appropri-

Figure 5.1. Intersections of identity and practice at St. Margaret's Academy Elementary School

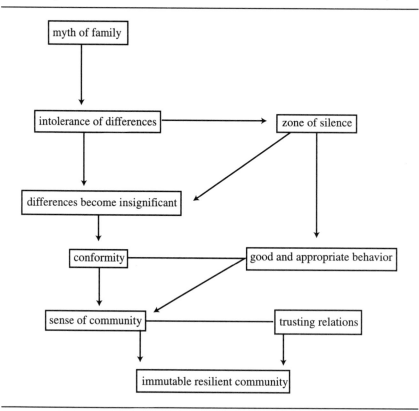

ate behavior and attitude. They took the notion of community for granted, considering it implicit in their family tradition. (See figure 5.2)

Why were the staff and students of Uptown School able to build resilient community, despite the many vulnerabilities opened by their practices? The answer lies in their trust in themselves and in each other to consistently live up to the values and ideals that drew them together. They could not refer to community longevity but instead looked to their everyday practices to affirm community and a sense of community. Although the staff and students at Uptown School devoted much time to academic pursuits, they also spent much time attending to the socialization of the students. Unlike that of the Catholic schools, however, Uptown's focus was not to normalize the students into specific patterns of behavior but rather to respond sensitively and wisely to the needs of the students. There was usually a reasonable match between their values and prac-

Figure 5.2. Intersections of identity and practice at St. Margaret's Academy High School

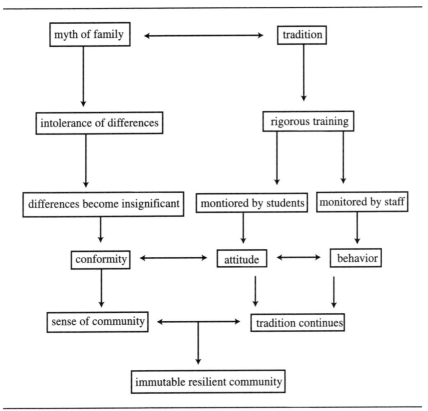

tices. Uncomfortable mismatches were conscientiously explored by staff and students in a whole-hearted pursuit of ideal community. (See figure 5.3)

Why did the building of resilient community fail in the remedial writing class? Resistance to forming community persisted because of existing in-group antipathies well founded in important sociopolitical patterns, the lack of understanding of the importance of the group's marginalization to Urban U's identity, and a deep reluctance to accept new identities cemented in stigma were only some of the reasons. In addition, the seduction of the notion of communal caring blotted out other reasonable pedagogical decisions, such as enforcing the use of writing workshop sessions.

There was no cohering set of values and little occasion for leadership; their central identity was fictive and never took hold, unlike the fictive aspects of identity at St. Margaret's.

There was a promise made to the students that together they would become better writers, real writers. But this was an impossible promise to keep,

Figure 5.3. Intersections of identity and practice at Uptown

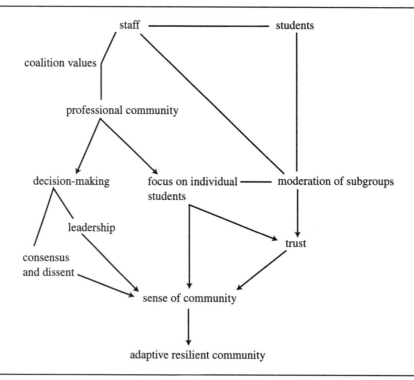

given the constraints of the institution that would force them to take a Writing Assessment Test that would not allow them to be a community of writers, and given their own lack of practice at writing. They found themselves in a double bind (Bateson, 1972). Unlike the classic double bind from which there is no escape, however, they could remove one of the conflicting conditions. So they gave up the promise of community, realizing that they had constructed an unlikely dream.

Throughout the semester, the teachers acted in ways that they believed would help the students pass the writing exam. Implicit in their plans for the students, however, was the realistic expectation that most of the students would not pass the WAT at the end of the semester. Their fluency in written standard English would continue to be judged insufficient by the anonymous examiners, who did not have access to the discussions that revealed ability to communicate and analyze complex ideas and arguments. As McDermott (1988) illuminates, the context of the test within the confines of the institution had always rendered them inarticulate and would continue to do so. In other words, they would not be able to write in a manner that the institution would recognize as valid.

As seen earlier, the teachers worked hard to create conditions that would support a sense of community among the students as they struggled to become better writers. They did create a narrative of shared identity, history, goals, and so on. They did learn how to be in community. They did attend to their own differences, and they did celebrate a sense of being in community. They engaged, if only briefly, in the central practice of a community of writers. Although each of these conditions was met at some time during the semester, only the forging of a sense of common experience with struggle and hardship was thoroughly developed. The development of a shared identity from this common experience with struggle was an important theme in every class meeting, but there is no evidence that the students believed in this common identity.

In addition, even when conditions supportive of community were called into existence, the group did not attend to their vulnerabilities in ways that supported community. Rather, they relied upon the shaky bonds of their moments of community to erase their vulnerability as failed writers. They called upon and celebrated an identity as struggling writers, an identity built not from sustained practice but from wishful thinking. They looked to the adjectives (struggling, failed, real) rather than the noun (writers) to define themselves. They were seduced by the lure and promise of community but did not recognize or enter into the very real contract that would have given a viable core to their group identity of struggling—but real—writers. They did not write together as their central practice.

In addition to the over-reliance on the transformative power of community, the group ignored the fragile nature of such possible transformation. For example, although transformation of stigma into honor can create valued identities, valued identities can, and did, co-exist with stigmatized identity. The identity of struggling writer, for example, necessitated a maintenance of the identity of failed writer at its core. Although critical analysis of situated lives is a potentially transformative act, realistic assessment of situated lives can result in resignation. The pain and anguish of the students during the writing test testifies to this. The magical thinking that led to the over-reliance on the transformative power of community was understandable, given the many disheartening failures at the WAT previously experienced by the students. The teachers' hope that a sense of community coupled with destigmatized identities as writers would carry at least some of the students successfully through the WAT is also understandable. They knew that these students were intelligent people who deserved an opportunity to earn a college degree. They understood their frustrations and sense of helplessness. They themselves were frustrated at their own failures to transform these and other struggling students into university-approved writers. They were willing to try any approach that might work.

But the responsibility for the unhappy trajectory of these struggling writers is not theirs alone. Identity that is forced upon a group has a greater likelihood to take hold if the group is willing to accept the identity and to change its beliefs and practices to safeguard it. However, alternative identities may not take hold if the dominant interpretation is effectively maintained. Marginalization is a powerful force, especially when constructed in such a way that the group cannot shed the stigma that supports the marginalization, particularly when the stigma is the central and cohering reason the group has come into existence. This group was acquired by its stigma (McDermott, 1994), a stigma that was an important element to the coherence of the larger college community that marginalized incompetent writers (Magolda & Knight-Abowitz, 1997). Urban U. only tentatively held a cohesive identity as a successful liberal arts college and sought to increase its status among other local colleges and universities. Significant numbers of students who were failing writers would validate poor public opinion of the college's reputation. In fact, the dominant reason that the college made any effort toward educating such misfits was in acknowledgment of its long history of providing higher education to the otherwise disenfranchised. However, the nature and scope of the services needed exploded exponentially during the late 1960s, a time when the college opened its doors as an expression of affirmative action. By the early 1990s, the college's image of success had eroded as its student population grew to include significant numbers of students requiring remediation in reading and writing English. It was in the service of shoring up its increasingly tarnished image that the WAT, manifestly an assessment designed to place students in appropriate classes, became an arbiter of who was entitled to receive a college education and degree. (See figure 5.4)

Figure 5.4. Intersections of identity and practice in remedial writing class

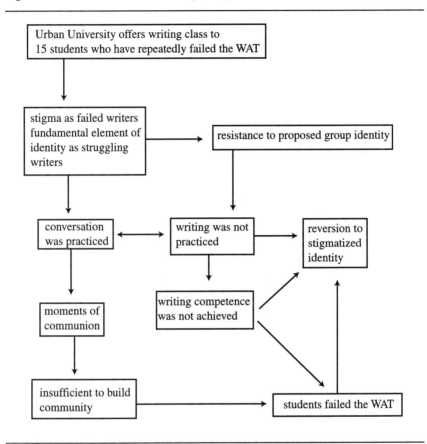

IMPLICATIONS FOR THE ROLE OF COMMUNITY IN EDUCATION

The data from this study and from the associated studies that provide its foundation do support the belief that being in community is valued and desired by people working together in schools. Their belief in community had real consequences for the groups in this study. Some consequences spell the story of family and tradition, others of democracy and transformation, and still others of vulnerability and disappointment.

The social relations of community are vulnerable and delicate. They bruise and falter easily. They require constant nurturing and defense from danger.

Because the potential dangers emanate from both inside and outside the social group, those who are or who would be within community must vigilantly maintain their protective guard. This guardedness exists in uneasy tension with the trusting relations considered so essential by the participants at the four sites. This is an irreducible tension that requires constant accommodation by those who would be in community.

The risk of fracture is real. The courage to risk the possible fractures is partially constituted by the hope that community is resilient. As mentioned before, the robustness or fragility of community may be measured by the community's ability to tolerate fractures while maintaining collective strengths, but its resilience may also depend upon the concurrence of two apparent contradictions: reduction of the possibilities of avoidable fractures and the sufficient occurrence of necessary vulnerable moments. The tolerable balance between these contradictions is not necessarily predictable across or within groups.

Because vulnerabilities are not static or stable within any group's process of community, it is not possible to concoct a clearly bounded set of practices guaranteed to support resilient community in schools. In addition, because the nurturing of the social relations and feelings about these that are recognizable as those of community are done in tandem with other practices that may or may not be done in order to support community, there is no list of practices that can be guaranteed to promote social relations and feelings that conjure community. Passionate arguments, for example, may generate a sense of community in one setting and not another, or at one moment and not another, within the same group (Myerhoff, 1978).

Commonality in community may be desired, even necessary, but maintaining important differences may be equally necessary. Transforming difference into commonality may seem to promise connection and commitment, but the hidden or unexpected price of this transformation may undermine the gains thus made. The accommodation of difference and its balance with sufficient commonality requires much time- and energy-consuming attention. This indicates that the central practice of the group—for example, writing—cannot be the only practice of the group.

The conditions for community cannot be successfully met serially or sporadically if community is to thrive within a group. The conditions must be continually called into existence through the interactions of the group and through its interaction with those outside the group. These conditions are mutually constitutive, each relying on the presence of the others to come into full flower. Given the evidence from the four groups, these conditions for community may best be supported through practices that are only secondarily designed to call up community, such as learning how to become a competent ninth grader, teaching explicitly, making wise decisions, and so on. In addition, the conditions may most effectively support the development of resilient community if they are cohesive, if they hold together with integral logic. Much of the vulnerability within community, as we have seen, is visible within the accommodations that must be made so that cohesiveness can result. Work undertaken by the group members to reduce inconsistencies among the necessary conditions, however, may or may not result in resilient community. Because the inconsistencies arise under different conditions, and have different histories that must be considered, the kinds of work that can be done to increase cohesiveness among the necessary conditions are always particular to a group. Sometimes the effectiveness of the work done is mitigated by factors outside the control of the group, as we saw happen to our struggling writers.

Critical examination of everyday practices may well support community in groups that place a premium on internal democracy, or that seek to transform schooling in general. Such critical examination fits well at Uptown, for example. Recent research aimed at transformation of urban schools has focused on the development of what are being called communities of inquiry (Fine, 1994; Lieberman, 1994; Vanderslice & Farmer, 1994; Waff, 1994). The term "community of inquiry" echoes Bryk et al.'s (1993) description of a school that "sees itself as a community that respects the dignity of each person, where members are free to question within a commitment to genuine dialogue . . ." (p. 299). In the service of this demand, Tinder (1980) examines the concept of inquiry, distinguishing two modes: inquiring about and inquiring with. Inquiring with others "is in itself community" (p. 24).

But inquiring about the social relations and practices that indicate community can be risky business for some groups, even though ignoring the fragility or vulnerability of community that exists or arises as the social relations and practices play out can also be risky. Critical examination of everyday practices may or may not undermine community in schools that have established traditional identity and practices that are deemed successful by the group. The uncertainty of what might replace cherished notions and firmly planted practices is not unreasonably feared by groups who believe that their actions are in satisfactory accord with their beliefs. Because this attitude allows such groups to carry out their primary practices effectively, they have little incentive to open the Pandora's box of critical inquiry. The decision to miss out on the positive possibilities of transformation is also a decision to avoid the negative possibilities of transformation.

The questions and challenges for remedial education brought to light by this study are currently of significant interest to Urban U. and to other colleges faced with the most recent public discontent with large-scale remedial programs in 4-year colleges. Evidence from this study might be cited by impatient administrators and legislators to demonstrate the ineffectiveness of remedial classes. Certainly, it is difficult to regard a pass rate of 2 students out of 15 as evidence of a successful endeavor, especially considering the expensive resources (two teachers, sign language interpreters, use of the ENFI system) employed. Yet there is something to learn about community and its role in successful remediation from this class.

For example, if the social relations of community are a positive influence on academic success, then these social relations should include not only the building of an identity as a community of practice but also sufficient opportunity for the members to work at their practice. Forty-five, sixty, or even seventy-five hours of class time over one semester may be too short a period to develop both community and practice for the neediest of populations. We, the public, and we, as faculty, administrators, and legislators, must decide whether to continue or to change the conditions under which students labor in remediation. Can we afford to give our students the time and resources they need to become successful members in a community of writers? Can we afford not to do so (Calderwood, in press-b)?

In addition, glossing over or ignoring the vulnerabilities or fragilities of the group did not support resilient community for our struggling writers. They and the teachers negotiated almost every session so that the students did not have time to write. Even ENFI discussions, relaxed and enjoyable, were avoided about half the time. They talked about struggles with writing but did not struggle to write. They spoke of their writing failures as if they were remnants of past experience but did not replace these threadbare remnants with new experiences as writers. Individuals and the institutions within which they operate must own up to their respective accountabilities and responsibilities. Institutional or personal changes in attitudes or practices cannot begin or continue in isolation from each other. Students and teachers can demand, and perhaps receive, adequate resources and time to become proficient, but they must make good use of these.

Would more of the students have passed the WAT if they had, indeed, become a resilient community of writers? This question can be answered with hope or despair but not with certainty. The students no longer struggle together.

But St. Margaret's Academy Elementary and High Schools and Uptown School continued their work of educating students successfully (Blot & Calderwood, 1995). Their success in this endeavor simultaneously facilitated and was facilitated by the resilience of community. Although their vulnerabilities differed, and although they attended to or ignored these vulnerabilities in their own quite different ways, they managed to successfully maintain a balanced relationship among the vulnerability, fragility, and resilience of community. They strove, each in their own fashion, to meet the ideals or traditions of community as they knew it.

Community that seeks to transform schooling may not be possible or even desired in every educative group. Such community, as we have seen at Uptown, is threaded with almost as much fragility as resilience. Normalizing, tradition-honoring community minimizes the occurrence of fragility more emphatically. However, adaptive resilient community may be more effective in transforming fragility into resilience. Whether adaptive or immutable community is possible, of course, greatly depends on institutional factors that may or may not be easily challenged. Despite these challenges, people will still seek to establish community in schools.

Groups that are well satisfied that community is strongly established in their schools may choose not to examine it too closely. However, those choosing to examine the nature of community and those seeking to establish community in schools might adapt the following set of questions: Why do we desire to be in community? What functions might community serve for the group? What effects would the presence of communal relations have on the central practices of the group? What effects will the central practices of the group have on community? How will we account for identity and diversity? How will we learn and teach each other to be in community? How will we celebrate ourselves in community? How will we respond to our vulnerabilities? How much fragility can we bear? How will we transform our vulnerabilities and fragilities into resilience? How will we know when we are in or out of community? Even groups that find critical inquiry dangerous or irrelevant can manage such reflection in the service of building ever more resilient community.

References

American Association of University Women Educational Foundation. (1993). *Hostile hallways: The AAUW survey on sexual harassment in America's schools.* Washington, D.C.: Author.

Anderson, B. (1991). *Imagined communities: Reflections on the origin and spread of nationalism* (Rev. ed.). London: Verso.

Atwell, N. (1987). *In the middle: Writing, reading and learning with adolescents.* Portsmouth, NH: Heinemann.

Bakhtin, M. M. (1981). Discourse in the novel. In *The dialogic imagination* (pp. 259–422). Austin: University of Texas Press.

Balin, J. (1994). Community and contagion: A neighborhood reception to a nursing home for people with AIDS. Unpublished doctoral dissertation, University of Pennsylvania, Philadelphia.

Barth, F. (1969). *Ethnic groups and boundaries: The social organization of culture difference.* Boston: Little, Brown.

Basso, K. H. (1972). "To give up on words": Silence in western Apache culture. In P. P. Giglioli (Ed.), *Language and social context* (pp. 67–86). New York: Penguin.

Bateson, G. (1972). *Steps to an ecology of mind.* San Francisco: Chandler.

Bellah, R. N., Madsen, R., Sullivan, W. M., Swindler, A., & Tipton, S. M. (1985). *Habits of the heart. Individualism and commitment in American life.* New York: Harper & Row.

Blot, R. K., & Calderwood, P. E. (1995). *The cultural construction of success in Catholic and public schools: Executive summary.* A project of The Facilitator Center, Pace University, New York.

Bourdieu, P. (1984). *Distinction: A social critique of the judgment of taste.* Cambridge, MA: Harvard University Press.

Boyd, D. (1996). Dominance concealed through diversity: Implications of inadequate perspectives on cultural pluralism. *Harvard Educational Review, 66*(3), 609–630.

Brehm, S. S., & Kassin, S. M. (1990). *Social psychology.* Boston: Houghton Mifflin.

Bryk, A. S., Lee, V. E., & Holland, P. B. (1993). *Catholic schools and the common good.* Cambridge, MA: Harvard University Press.

Calderwood, P. (1997). *Understanding community: A comparison of the tasks of community in four school settings.* Unpublished doctoral dissertation, University of Pennsylvania, Philadelphia.

Calderwood, P. (1998a). Apart together: "Girl talk" and "boy talk" classes at an urban middle school. *Urban Education, 33*(2), 243–263.

Calderwood, P. (1998b). A review of discipline, moral regulation, and schooling: A social history. *Educational Studies, 29*(2), 171–175.

Calderwood, P. (in press-a). The decision dance: Staff decision making in a restructuring urban middle school. *The Urban Review*.

Calderwood, P. (in press-b). When community fails to transform: Raveling and unraveling a community of writers. *The Urban Review*.

Cohen, A. (1985). *The symbolic construction of community*. London: Routledge.

Cohen, A. (1994). *Self consciousness: An alternative anthropology of identity*. London: Routledge.

Coleman, J. S., & Hoffer, T. (1987). *Public and private high schools: The impact of communities*. New York: Basic Books.

Conway, J. A. (1985). A perspective on organizational cultures and organizational belief structure. *Educational Administration Quarterly, 21*(4), 7–25.

Csikszentmihalyi, M. (1995). Toward an evolutionary hermeneutics: The case of wisdom. In R. Goodman & W. Fisher (Eds.), *Rethinking knowledge: Reflections across the disciplines* (pp. 123–143). Albany: State University of New York Press.

Cuba, L. (1993). A place to call home: Identification with dwelling, community and region. *The Sociological Quarterly, 34*(1), 111–131.

Delpit, L. D., (1993). The silenced dialogue: Power and pedagogy in educating other people's children. In M. Fine & L. Weis (Eds.), *Beyond silenced voices* (pp. 119–139). Albany: State University of New York Press.

Deutch, M. (1990). Psychological roots of moral exclusion. *Journal of Social Issues, 46*(1), 21–26.

Dewey, J. (1969). The search for the great community. In D. Minar & S. Greer (Eds.), *The concept of community: Readings with interpretations* (pp. 333–338). Chicago: Aldine.

Dewey, J. (1990). *The school and society. The child and the curriculum*. Chicago: University of Chicago Press. (Original work published 1900)

Dorman, G. (1987). *Improving middle-grades schools: A framework for action*. Carrboro, NC: Center for Early Adolescence.

Epstein, C. Fuchs. (1992). Tinkerbells and pinups: The construction and reconstruction of gender boundaries at work. In M. Lamont & M. Fournier (Eds.), *Cultivating differences: Symbolic boundaries and the making of inequality* (pp. 232–256). Chicago: University of Chicago Press.

Erickson, F. (1987). Transformation and school success: The politics and culture of educational achievement. *Anthropology and Education Quarterly, 18*(4), 335–382.

Etzioni, A. (1993). *The spirit of community*. New York: Simon & Schuster.

Fine, M. (1987). Silencing in public schools. *Language Arts, 64*(2), 157–171.

Fine, M. (1990). "The public" in public schools: The social construction/constriction of moral communities. *Journal of Social Issues, 46*(1), 107–120.

Fine, M. (Ed.). (1994). *Chartering urban school reform: Reflections on public high schools in the midst of change*. New York: Teachers College Press.

Fordham, S. (1988). Racelessness as a factor in black students' school success: Pragmatic strategy or Pyrrhic victory. *Harvard Educational Review, 58*(1), 54–84.

Foresta, C. (1996). Reflections on ice-skating. In M. Fine (Ed.), *Talking across borders: Participatory evaluation research in an urban middle school* (pp. 19–21). New York: The Bruner Foundation.

Frazer, E., & Lacey, N. (1993). *The politics of community: A feminist critique of the liberal communitarian debate.* Toronto: University of Toronto Press.

Freire, P. (1985). *The politics of education: Culture, power and liberation.* Westport, CT: Bergin & Garvey.

Freire, P., & Macedo, D. (1987). *Literacy. Reading the word and the world.* Westport, CT: Bergin & Garvey.

Gans, H. (1992). Preface. In M. Lamont & M. Fournier (Eds.), *Cultivating differences: Symbolic boundaries and the making of inequality* (pp. vii–xvi). Chicago: University of Chicago Press.

Giles, H. (1995, August). *Fostering resilience in urban minority parents: Social capital and racial identity in parent-school collaboration.* Paper presented at the 103rd convention of the American Psychological Association, New York.

Ginsberg, C. (1994). Killing a Chinese mandarin: The moral implications of distance. *Critical Inquiry, 21*(1), 46–60.

Glare, P. E. W. (1990). *The Oxford Latin Dictionary.* Oxford: Oxford Clarenden Press.

Glasman, N. (1994). *Making better decisions about school problems.* Thousand Oaks, CA: Sage.

Goffman, E. (1959). *The presentation of self in everyday life.* New York: Doubleday.

Goffman, E. (1961). *Asylum: Essays on the social situation of mental patients and other inmates.* New York: Doubleday.

Goffman, E. (1963a). *Behavior in public places: Notes on the social organization of gatherings.* New York: The Free Press.

Goffman, E. (1963b). *Stigma: Notes on the management of spoiled identity.* New York: Simon & Schuster.

Graves, S. (1995, August). *Psychological support of low-performing schools: The Accelerated Schools Project.* Paper presented at the 103rd convention of the American Psychological Association, New York.

Gumperz, J. (1972). Verbal strategies in multilingual communication. In R. Abrahams & R. Troike (Eds.), *Language and cultural diversity in American education* (pp. 184–195). Englewood Cliffs, NJ: Prentice Hall.

Gusfield, J. R. (1975). *Community: A critical response.* New York: Harper & Row.

Harding, S. (1991). *Whose science? Whose knowledge? Thinking from women's lives.* Ithaca, NY: Cornell University Press.

Harding, S. (1995). Subjectivity, experience, and knowledge: An epistemology from/for rainbow coalition politics. In J. Roof & R. Wiegman (Eds.), *Who can speak? Authority and critical identity* (pp. 120–136). Chicago: University of Illinois Press.

Hemmings, A. (1996). Conflicting images? Being black and a model high school student. *Anthropology and Education Quarterly, 27*(1), 20–50.

Henry, J. (1968). Docility, or giving the teacher what she wants. In J. Chilcott, N. Greenberg, & H. Wilson (Eds.), *Readings in the socio-cultural foundations of education* (pp. 248–256). Belmont, CA: Wadsworth.

Hillary, G. A. (1955). Definitions of community: Areas of agreement. *Rural Sociology, 20*(1), 111, 123.

Hillary, G. A. (1959). A critique of selected community concepts. *Social Forces, 37,* 237–242.

Hillary, G. A. (1986). *Communal organizations: A study of local societies.* Chicago: University of Chicago Press.

Hymes, D. (1972a). Models of the interaction of language and social life. In J. Gumperz & D. Hymes (Eds.), *Directions in sociolinguistics* (pp. 35–71). New York: Basil Blackwell.

Hymes, D. (1972b). On communicative competence. In J. B. Pride & J. Holmes (Eds.), *Sociolinguistics* (pp. 269–293). New York: Penguin.

Johnson, D., & Johnson, F. (1987). *Joining together: Group theory and group skills.* Englewood Cliffs, NJ: Prentice Hall.

Jones, E. E., & Nisbett, R. E. (1972). The actor and the observer: Divergent perceptions of the causes of behavior. In E. E. Jones, D. D. Kanouse, H. H. Kelley, R. E. Nisbett, S. Valins, & B. Weiner (Eds.), *Attribution: Perceiving the causes of behavior* (pp. 79–94). Morristown, NJ: General Learning Press.

Kihlstrom, J., Marchese-Foster, L., & Klein, S. (1997). Situating the self in interpersonal space. In U. Neisser & D. Jopling (Eds.), *The conceptual self in context: Culture, experience, self-understanding* (pp. 54–175). Cambridge: Cambridge University Press.

Knight-Abowitz, K. (1997). Neglected aspects of the liberal-communitarian debate and implications for school communities. *Educational Foundations, 11*(2), 63–82.

Labov, W. (1982). Objectivity and commitment in linguistic science: The case of the black English Trial in Ann Arbor. *Language in Society, 11,* 165–201.

Lather, P. (1991). *Getting smart: Feminist research and pedagogy with/in the postmodern.* New York: Routledge.

Lave, J., & Wenger, E. (1991). *Situated Learning: Legitimate peripheral participation.* Cambridge: Cambridge University Press.

Lee, V. E., Bryk, A. S., & Smith, J. B. (1993). The organization of effective secondary schools. *Review of Research in Education, 19,* 171–267.

Licata, J. W., Teddlie, C. B., & Greenfield, W. D. (1990). Principal vision, teacher sense of autonomy, and environmental robustness. *Journal of Educational Research, 84*(2), 93—99.

Lieberman, A. (1992). The meaning of scholarly activity and the building of community. *Educational Researcher, 21*(6), 5–12.

Lieberman, A. (1994). Afterword: Transforming urban schools: Building knowledge and building community. In M. Fine (Ed.), *Chartering urban school reform: Reflections on public high schools in the midst of change* (pp. 204–207). New York: Teachers College Press.

Lipsitz, J. (1984). *Successful schools for young adolescents.* New Brunswick, NJ: Transaction Books.

Long, M., & Porter, P. (1985). Group work, interlanguage talk, and second language acquisition. *TESOL Quarterly, 19*(2), 207–228.

Louis, K. S., & Kruse, S. D. (Eds.). (1995). *Professionalism and community: Perspectives on urban school reform.* Thousand Oaks, CA: Corwin Press.

Magolda, P., & Knight-Abowitz, K. (1997). Communities and tribes in residential living. *Teachers College Record, 99*(2), 266–310.

Mandelbaum, S. J. (1988). Open moral communities. *Society, 26*(1), 20–27.

Mansbridge, J. (1996). Using power/fighting power: The polity. In S. Benhabib (Ed.), *Democracy and difference: Contesting the boundaries of the political* (pp. 46–66). Princeton, NJ: Princeton University Press.

Maslow, A. (1962). *Toward a psychology of being.* Princeton, NJ: Van Nostrand.

McDermott, R. P. (1977). Social relations as contexts for learning in schools. *Harvard Educational Review, 47*(2), 198–213.

McDermott, R. P. (1988). Inarticulateness. In D. Tannen (Ed.), *Linguistics in context: Connecting observation and understanding* (pp. 37–69). Norwood, NJ: Ablex.

McDermott, R. P. (1994). The acquisition of a child by a learning disability. In J. Lave & S. Chaiklin (Eds.), *Understanding practice: Perspectives on activity and content* (pp. 269–305). Cambridge: Cambridge University Press.

McLaren, P. (1986). Making Catholics: The ritual production of conformity in a Catholic junior high school. *Journal of Education, 168*(2), 55–77.

McQuillan, P., & Muncie, D. (1994). "Change takes time": A look at the growth and development of the Coalition of Essential Schools. *Journal of Curriculum Studies, 26*(3), 265–279.

Mead, G. H. (1934). *Mind, self, and society from the standpoint of a social behaviorist.* Chicago: University of Chicago Press.

Mews, S. (1971). Community as a sociological concept. In L. Bright (Ed.), *The Christian community: Essays on the role of the Church in the world* (pp. 1–48). London: Sheed & Ward.

Mijuskovic, B. (1992). Organic communities, atomistic societies, and loneliness. *Journal of Sociology and Social Welfare, 19*(2), 147–164.

Minar, D., & Greer, S. (Eds.). (1969). *The concept of community: Readings with interpretations.* Chicago: Aldine.

Minow, M. (1990). *Making all the difference: Inclusion, exclusion and American law.* Ithaca, NY: Cornell University Press.

Moon, J. D. (1993). *Constructing community: Moral pluralism and tragic conflicts.* Princeton, NJ: Princeton University Press.

Moore, D. (1992). The case for parent and community involvement. In G.A. Hess (Ed.), *Empowering teachers and parents: School restructuring through the eyes of anthropologists* (pp. 131–156). Westport, CT: Bergin & Garvey.

Muncie, D., & McQuillan, P. (1992). The dangers of assuming a consensus for change: Some examples from the Coalition of Essential Schools. In G. A. Hess (Ed.), *Empowering teachers and parents: School restructuring through the eyes of anthropologists* (pp. 47–69). Westport, CT: Bergin & Garvey.

Muncie, D., & McQuillan, P. (1993). Education reform as revitalization movement. *American Journal of Education, 101*, 393–431.

Myerhoff, B. (1978). *Number our days.* New York: Simon & Schuster.

National Middle School Association. (1982). *This we believe.* Columbus, OH: Author.

Newmann, F., Rutter, R., & Smith, M. (1989). Organizational factors that affect school sense of efficacy, community, and expectations. *Sociology of Education, 62*, 221–238.

Nisbet, R. A. (1953). *The quest for community: A study in the ethics of order and freedom*. Oxford: Oxford University Press.

Oakes, J., Quartz, K. H., Gong, J., Guiton, G., & Lipton, M. (1993). Creating middle schools: Technical, normative, and political considerations. *Elementary School Journal, 93*(5), 461–480.

Opotow, S. (1990). Moral exclusion and injustice: An introduction. *Journal of Social Issues, 46*(1), 1–20.

Padden, C., & Humphries, T. (1988). *Deaf in America: Voices from a culture*. Cambridge, MA: Harvard University Press.

Phillips, D. L. (1993). *Looking backward: A critical appraisal of communitarian thought*. Princeton, NJ: Princeton University Press.

Puddifoot, J. E. (1993). Community identity and sense of belonging in a northeastern English town. *The Journal of Social Psychology, 134*(5), 601–608.

Purpel, D. (1989). *The moral and spiritual crisis in education: A curriculum for justice and compassion in education*. Granby, MA: Bergin & Garvey.

Robertson, B. A. (1995, August). *Self-identification as disabled: Underlying perspectives*. Paper presented at the 103rd annual convention of the American Psychological Association, New York.

Robinson, A. (1994). It takes one to know one: Passing and communities of common interest. *Critical Inquiry, 20*(4), 715–736.

Rosenholtz, S. (Ed.). (1989). *Teachers' workplace: The social organization of schools*. New York: Longman.

Rousmaniere, K., Dehli, K., & de Coninck-Smith, N. (Eds.). (1997). *Discipline, moral regulation, and schooling: A social history*. New York & London: Garland.

Sansom, B. (1982). The sick who do not speak. In D. Parkin (Ed.), *Semantic anthropology* (pp. 183–195). London: Academic Press.

Schon, D. (1995). Causality and causal inference in the study of organizations. In R. Goodman & W. Fisher (Eds.), *Rethinking knowledge: Reflections across the disciplines* (pp. 69–102). Albany: State University of New York Press.

Schwartz, A. (1990, April). *School social context, teacher culture, and school-based management*. Paper presented at the annual meeting of the American Educational Research Association, Boston, MA.

Schwartz, S. H. (1994). Are there universal aspects in the structure and contents of human values? *Journal of Social Issues, 50*(4), 19–45.

Sergiovanni, T. J. (1994). *Building community in schools*. San Francisco: Jossey-Bass.

Sherif, M., Harvey, L. J., White, B. J., Hood, W. R., & Sherif, C. W. (1988). *The Robber Cave experiment: Intergroup conflict and cooperation*. Middletown, CT: Wesleyan University Press.

Shor, I. (1989). Developing student autonomy in the classroom. *Equity & Excellence, 24*(3), 35–39.

Sibley, D. (1995). *Geographies of exclusion: Society and difference in the west*. London: Routledge.

Sizer, T. (1992). *Horace's school: Redesigning the American high school*. New York: Houghton Mifflin.

Smiley, M. (1992). *Moral responsibility and the boundaries of community: Power and accountability from a pragmatic point of view*. Chicago: University of Chicago Press.

Sola, M., & Bennett, A. T. (1985). The struggle for voice: Narrative, literacy and consciousness in an East Harlem school. *Journal of Education, 167*(1), 88–109.

Staessens, K. (1991, April). *The professional culture of innovating primary schools: Nine case studies.* Paper presented at the annual meeting of the American Educational Research Association, Chicago, IL.

Stein, M. R. (1960). *The eclipse of community; an interpretation of American studies.* Princeton, NJ: Princeton University Press.

Tannen, D. (1994). *Gender and discourse.* New York: Oxford University Press.

Tinder, G. (1980). *Community: Reflections on a tragic ideal.* Baton Rouge: Louisiana State University Press.

Tönnies, F. (1988). *Community and society (Gemeinschaft und Gesellschaft)* (J. Samples, Ed.). New Brunswick: Transaction Books. (Original work published 1887)

Vanderberghe, R., & Staessens, K. (1991, April). *Vision as a core component in school culture.* Paper presented at the annual meeting of the American Educational Research Association, Chicago, IL.

Vanderslice, V. (1995). Cooperation within a competitive context. In B. Bunker & J. Rubin (Eds.), *Conflict, cooperation, and justice: Essays inspired by the work of Morton Deutsch* (pp. 175–204). San Francisco: Jossey Bass.

Vanderslice, V., & Farmer, S. (1994). Transforming ourselves: Becoming an inquiring community. In M. Fine (Ed.), *Chartering urban school reform: Reflections on public high schools in the midst of change* (pp. 85–97). New York: Teachers College Press.

Volosinov, V. N. (1973). *Marxism and the philosophy of language.* Cambridge, MA: Harvard University Press.

Vroom, V. H., & Yetton, P. W. (1973). *Leadership and decision-making.* Pittsburgh, PA: University of Pittsburgh Press.

Waff, D. (1994). Girl talk: Creating community through social exchange. In M. Fine (Ed.), *Chartering urban school reform: Reflections on public high schools in the midst of change* (pp. 192–203). New York: Teachers College Press.

Warren, R. P. (1969). Leadership from the periphery. In D. Minar & S. Greer (Eds.), *The concept of community: Readings with interpretations* (pp. 339–356). Chicago: Aldine.

Wertsch J. (1991). *Voices of the mind.* Cambridge, MA: Harvard University Press.

Westheimer, J (1998). *Among schoolteachers.* New York: Teachers College Press.

Williams, R. (1976). *Keywords. A vocabulary of culture and society.* New York: Oxford University Press.

Wolfe, A. (1992). Democracy versus sociology: Boundaries and their political consequences. In M. Lamont & M. Fournier (Eds.), *Cultivating differences: Symbolic boundaries and the making of inequality* (pp. 309–326). Chicago: University of Chicago Press.

Yetton, P., & Crawford, M. (1992). Reassessment of participative decision-making: A case of too much participation. In F. Heller (Ed.), *Decision-making and leadership* (pp. 90–111). Cambridge: Cambridge University Press.

Young, I. M. (1990). *Justice and the politics of difference.* Princeton, NJ: Princeton University Press.

Index

About the Author

Patricia Calderwood is an assistant professor of curriculum and instruction at the Graduate School of Education and Allied Professions at Fairfield University, in Fairfield, Connecticut. Previously, she taught as an adjunct and then as a substitute assistant professor of education at Lehman College of the City University of New York. She earned an M.S.Ed. in reading from Lehman College in 1989, and a Ph.D. in Education, Culture, and Society from the University of Pennsylvania in 1997. She specializes in qualitative research methodologies, teacher education, language and literacy socialization, and issues of community. Her current work examines the long-term sustainability of resilient community in schools and other organizations. Some of her recent publications appear in *At A Crossroads: Participatory Evaluation Research in a Restructuring Urban Middle School*, M. Fine (Ed.), 1996, and in the journals *Urban Education* and *The Urban Review*. Just for fun, an examination of a child's song as egocentric speech appears in the *Early Childhood Education Journal*.